YOGA

YOGA

NOA BELLING

BARNES
&NOBLE
BOOKS
NEW YORK

This edition published by Barnes & Noble, Inc. by arrangement
with New Holland Publishers (U.K.) Ltd

2003 by Barnes & Noble Books

M 10 9 8 7 6 5 4 3 2 1

ISBN 0-7607-3942-0

Publishing Manager: Claudia Dos Santos
Managing Editor: Simon Pooley
Managing Art Editor: Richard MacArthur
Editor: Mariëlle Renssen
Designer: Sheryl Buckley
Illustrator: Alzette Prins & Steven Felmore
Photo Research: Bronwyn Allies
Production: Myrna Collins
Consultants: Simon Low (UK)
Carol Francis (South Africa)

Reproduction by Unifoto (Pty) Ltd
Printed and bound in Malaysia by Times Offset (M) Sdn. Bhd.

THIS BOOK IS
DEDICATED TO

The peace, health, and happiness
of all living beings.

CONTENTS

THE word "yoga" is derived from the Sanskrit language and means "to unite" or "to harmonize;" that is, Yoga is a means of working toward a level where the activities of the body, mind, and spirit function together harmoniously.

Yoga also refers to the union between the individual and something greater, whether it is called God, the divine, or anything else. Nevertheless, Yoga does not represent or promote any particular religion. It is a system that aims to help people achieve their full potential through a heightened consciousness. Using age-old techniques that are accessible to anyone who is interested, the postures work toward the development of every human faculty: physical, mental, emotional, and spiritual.

Introduction to Yoga

THE YOGIC SYSTEM

Yoga is often referred to as a science. It is a system that has many branches, each with its own focus and set of rules and ethics (universal ethical principles and rules of personal conduct). It was systemized 3000 years ago by the Hindu philosopher Patañjali. Elements that were referred to in these writings appear, in the form of 185 aphorisms, in Patañjali's famous detailed work *Yoga Sutras*, believed to have been written sometime between 400 and 200BC. This is still considered to be the definitive work on Yoga.

A psychological, physiological, and spiritual discipline that has been an integral part of Indian culture for thousands of years, ancient Yogis developed the yogic system because they believed that by working through the body and the breath, they could achieve mastery over the nature of the mind, their emotions, and general well-being.

The precise origins of Yoga remain somewhat of a mystery, since Yoga philosophy was passed down by oral tradition—received by sages through meditation. The first recorded mention of Yoga appears in a collection of Hindu scriptures called the *Vedas*, dating back to about 1500BC. However, archeological finds in the Indus Valley of intact ceramics depicting figures in yogic meditation poses show that Yoga was practiced at least 5000 years ago.

Yoga was introduced into the West by an Indian sage called Swami Vivekananda, who demonstrated Yoga postures at a World Fair in Chicago in the 1890s. This generated much interest and laid the grounds for the welcoming of many other Yogis and Swamis (Hindu religious teachers) from India in the years that followed. Today, Yoga thrives throughout the world. Yoga postures have infiltrated today's physical culture in a number of ways: they can be identified in aerobics, stretch, and strength routines and appear in or are adapted for dance, gymnastics, and sports warm-up routines.

Each of the many branches belonging to the science of Yoga focuses on a different means of achieving union of the individual soul with the universal soul, or the divine within—the greatness of human potential. The idea of the different branches is to accommodate all types of people. The focus of this book is on the branch known as Hatha Yoga, with a Raja Yoga (mastery of the mind) component included in the form of an introduction to meditation.

Above **Extraordinarily loose-limbed postures like this 18th-century gouache miniature indicate the natural suppleness of Hindus accustomed to sitting cross-legged on the floor.**

Hatha yoga

This system of Yoga works through mastery of the body. This is achieved by embodying experience on a sensory, physical level together with awareness of the breath. It is a practical branch of Yoga, a system of training that uses physical postures, breathing, and relaxation techniques, and it is the best known in the West. These techniques benefit the muscular and skeletal body as well as the nervous system, glands, and vital organs. The aim is to promote vibrant health by tapping into the body's latent energy reserves.

The term "hatha" is a compound word: "ha" means "sun" and "tha" means "moon," with the implication of coming together or the balancing of duality, manifested in so many ways: male and female, day and night, light and dark, stability and mobility, hot and cold, yin and yang—or any other opposite yet balancing pair.

As an applied concept, this refers to bringing both sides of the body into a state of dynamic balance, a balance between stability and mobility. This can be achieved through the development of strength and flexibility equally to both sides, and within, the body to allow it to function more efficiently and with greater poise. At the same time, Hatha Yoga influences the left and right hemispheres of the brain to function in balance, so that the logical, mathematical side and the creative, intuitive side are encouraged to work in harmony.

Some believe that the aim of this Yoga system is also to prepare body and mind for Raja Yoga, which works on enhancing consciousness—although on its own, Hatha Yoga also exerts an integrating influence over the mind and body.

Many of the Yoga postures have been adapted and simplified for the Western body, which may not have grown up accustomed to this practice. For example, in the West people are brought up to sit on chairs, whereas in India people are accustomed to sitting cross-legged or squatting. In Indian culture, children are often introduced to Yoga at a very young age, giving them a head start in flexibility.

For reasons such as these, it can take years of dedicated practice to achieve some of the more complex postures, thus necessitating levels of progression while learning Yoga. The tensions and pressures of modern life can also reduce flexibility and can inhibit one's ability to tap into and trust in the strength of inner resources.

Most schools and forms of Hatha Yoga adhere to certain basic elements of Yoga, with each having a slightly different slant on teaching and practice. Four common schools are Iyengar, Sivananda, Ashtanga, and Kundalini. Raja Yoga, on the other hand, works on achieving a union of mind and soul through mastering the mind. Considered to be the royal path of Yoga (the Sanskrit term "raja" means "king" or "supreme"), it involves mental disciplines that work toward stilling the mind's incessant

Above *Sadhus*, India's devout spiritual philosophers, practice Yoga religiously to aid their journey to enlightenment.

thought processes and mastering consciousness. More pre-cisely, this refers to the skill to develop acute awareness, first through concentration, which allows you to meditate. Then, once you are able to transcend all thoughts, this leads you into a superconscious state that enables you to tap into instinct and inner wisdom.

There are several other branches of Yoga besides Hatha and Raja—the result of varying interpretations of the differ-ent types of Yoga discussed in the ancient Hindu texts of the *Upanishads* and *Bhagavad Gita*, where individuals have emphasized particular aspects and founded schools based on their own interpretation. These include Jnana Yoga (gaining knowledge through the study of scriptures and meditation), Bhakti Yoga (works through love and ritualistic devotion to a deity, guru, or prophet), Karma Yoga (works on selfless action and service), Mantra Yoga (vocal or mental repetition of sacred sounds, believed to raise consciousness), and Laya or Kundalini Yoga (awakens and raises the body's latent psychic nerve-force, or kundalini, located below the navel area) through the chakra energy centers.

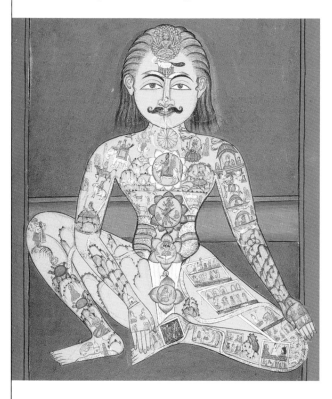

THE YOGIC VIEW OF HEALTH

Good health, according to Yoga philosophy, is influenced by a number of factors. These include regular exercise in the form of physical postures, proper breathing, sufficient rest and relaxation, meditation to cultivate mental focus and serenity, positive thinking, and a healthy, balanced diet. Yoga is one of the few systems that encompasses all of these components.

WELL-BEING AND HAPPINESS

Yoga is both a system for maintaining long-lasting health and cultivating a sense of happiness and fulfillment, and it encourages personal growth and development. It achieves this by teaching us how to tap into our inner energy reserves and generate health and well-being from within. True happi-ness cannot be bought—it is the result of a lifelong invest-ment in the self. According to Yoga philosophy, the state of the nerves, glands, and vital organs determines how healthy a person looks and feels. Regular Yoga practice will help to counter the accumulation of excess tension and the general physical decline due to negligent handling of the body or as a result of premature aging. Yoga therefore enhances both the youthfulness of the body and the clarity of the mind.

ENHANCED BODY AWARENESS

Yoga is a means of becoming more familiar with your body (both within and without). Its comprehensive system of exercise stretches, strengthens, tones, and helps to align the entire body. The different Yoga postures are together designed to benefit every anatomical structure, system, and organ of the body. This process of learning how to assist your

Left **A gouache of a tattooed Yogi shows the positioning of the chakras (subtle energy centers), which are balanced by practicing Yoga postures that soothe the endocrine and central nervous systems, thus benefitting the immune system.**

body in its healthy functioning can be empowering. And in developing a state of mental calmness and emotional stability, it offers guidelines to you to bring about changes in your physical, emotional, mental, and spiritual states, and to bring all four into balance and health.

STRESS RELIEF AND PREVENTION

Life today can be fast-paced, competitive, and stressful—although the benefits of moderate amounts of stress should not be ignored, as it can also be motivating, uplifting, and invigorating. Nevertheless, when the demands placed upon us greatly exceed our habitual levels of performance or ability to cope (whether physical, emotional, or mental), we suffer discomfort and strain, and the body's defenses become overworked and exhausted. Side effects may include frustration, muscular tension (that can contribute toward back problems), depression, anxiety, shortness of breath, and problems with concentration.

Yoga works first to relieve, then prevent such symptoms of stress affecting the body. Flexibility exercises are helpful in preventing or alleviating muscular tension in the first instance. Secondly, the use of controlled, deep breathing while executing each posture helps to counter any shortness or irregularity of breath associated with stress. This leads to a state of calmness and emotional stability, as the breath is closely linked to emotions and the state of your mind. Thirdly, the training in deep relaxation provides effective skills to cope with stress through control of the mind's chatter and attaining a stillness and mental clarity.

WHO CAN BENEFIT FROM YOGA?

Yoga is suitable for and beneficial to all ages and levels of fitness. Depending on the practitioner, it can be adapted from a very gentle form of exercise into a rigorous one. Regular Yoga practice can also be combined with other activities, such as visits to the gym, cardiovascular training programs, sports, or dance.

Focus of this book

- It introduces basic elements common to most schools of Yoga, without promoting any particular school of Yoga or any religion.
- It offers step-by-step guidance with clear progression from beginner postures to the slightly more advanced versions.
- It is suitable for all levels of fitness as it offers a number of versions for each posture, thus allowing for different degrees of flexibility and strength.
- It can be used in addition to attending Yoga classes to help you to practice safely at home, familiarize yourself with the names and your execution of the postures, and speed up your rate of improvement.
- It offers sample session ideas to help you get started in your practice on your own and as a demonstration of posture combination.

SANSKRIT TERMS IN YOGA

Sanskrit is an ancient Indo-European language that is linked to Latin, Greek, and Persian; early Hindus used it to record their scriptures, as well as philosophical and scientific texts.

The Yoga teaching tradition was originally an oral as opposed to a written one, and because it was esoteric in nature, has resulted in some degree of ambiguity in interpretation. For this reason, there may be differences in the names given to Yoga postures at different schools throughout the world. However, most schools do adhere to certain basic elements of Yoga, each with a slightly different slant on teaching and practice.

This book follows a commonly accepted system of posture naming, based on the studies and teachings of a number of Yoga teachers with various approaches.

CERTAIN *basic elements common to most schools of Yoga form the foundation upon which the rest of Yoga is built. These are: posture, breathing, relaxation, and meditation. These elements play an integral part in Hatha Yoga practice. For example, in executing a Yoga posture, breath awareness helps to minimize unnecessary tension as well as to help focus your attention in the present moment. Also, in all postures it is important to find a balance between relaxing or surrendering into the posture while being vitally aware and actively engaged in its execution. This balance can be achieved by making relaxation postures an integral part of your Yoga practice.*

THE BASIC ELEMENTS

INCORPORATING a regular meditation practice as part of your Yoga is crucial. Meditation trains you to have a sense of awareness through the ability to focus the mind's attention purely on the present moment—on the details and the physical sensation of the posture being executed. And regular Hatha Yoga practice can assist your ability to maintain a comfortable sitting position for an extended period of time, as is required for meditation. This is achieved through your work on improving body alignment, which then reduces unnecessary tension—your meditation practice would otherwise be hindered because of the body tiring sooner.

Below left The Sanskrit names of many Yoga asanas come from mythology, animals, and also refer to various parts of the body, so it is useful to familiarize yourself with these terms. A good example is the posture Utthita Hasta Padangusthasana, where *utthita* means extended, *hasta* is hand, *pada* is foot, and *padangustha* means thumb or toe.

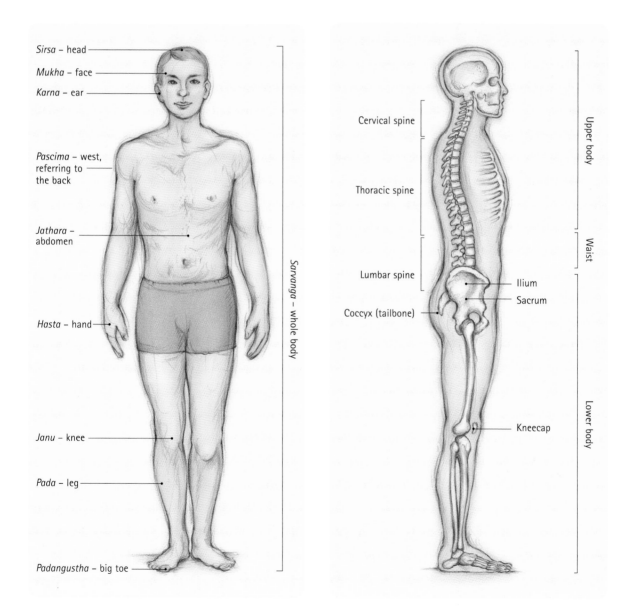

Sirsa – head
Mukha – face
Karna – ear
Pascima – west, referring to the back
Jathara – abdomen
Hasta – hand
Janu – knee
Pada – leg
Padangustha – big toe
Sarvanga – whole body

Cervical spine
Thoracic spine
Lumbar spine
Coccyx (tailbone)
Ilium
Sacrum
Kneecap
Upper body
Waist
Lower body

POSTURE

The starting point for all movement is posture—it is how the body is held in space. A healthy posture is one in which only the necessary amount of tension required by the muscles to support the upright body is present. A dynamic balance exists between being relaxed and feeling vitally alive.

The healthy posture involves symmetry between the two sides of the body and is facilitated by the proper alignment of the skeleton and muscular balance. It includes a lengthening upward from the waist, so that the head and upper body feel poised and light, accompanied by a sense of the legs and feet being well grounded, providing a stable foundation for the body. Breathing should be regular, easy, and should flow naturally.

In the event of an individual experiencing any anatomical imbalance such as scoliosis or an uneven leg length, the idea is to work toward enhancing the body's sense of balance and poise as much as possible.

The benefits of a balanced posture are numerous. The body can be used with increased awareness, flexibility, and energy, and the internal workings of the body function optimally. The life-force flows more freely throughout the body, increasing your sense of vitality. Relaxed breathing helps the flow of movement to become easier and freer. Because the skeletal structure is grounded and brought into better alignment, the nervous system perceives this stability and allows the muscles to release unnecessary tension.

This balanced poise is promoted through the practice of Yoga. By adopting different physical positions (referred to as Yoga postures—or in Sanskrit, as asanas), the body is opened up, toned, and strengthened. A naturally healthy posture also helps you to correctly execute the Yoga asanas, and can speed up your rate of improvement while enhancing the benefits that are gained through regular practice. You are less likely to injure yourself, too.

What follows are some basic standing and sitting positions, or asanas, designed to encourage a healthy alignment before you move on to more complex Yoga postures. These basic positions can be practiced independently to train you generally to adopt a daily healthy posture. They can be done in front of a mirror or—even better—with a partner who can give you feedback, to enable you to develop an awareness of where you should work on improving alignment and symmetry in your body.

Above **With the aid of a straight-backed chair as support, doing spinal twists while keeping the spine elongated will help to counteract the effect of many hours spent hunched over a desk or typing behind a computer.**

BASIC STANDING POSITION

TADASANA

the Mountain Pose

tada = mountain

asana = pose, posture

Tadasana can be included within a session, either as a preparation for standing postures or as a posture in its own right. It can also be used as a symmetrical counterposture to asymmetrical standing or balancing postures.

Tadasana is a development on Samasthiti, or steady pose, a poised and alive posture cultivating a sense of strength and stability. It is because of its stability—an important quality for any foundation—that Tadasana is useful as a starting position for standing postures and balances.

This pose is also effective in making you aware of how mind and imagination influence posture and balance. You will notice a natural tendency to sway while holding Tadasana. The idea is to gently control this tendency through mental focus, willpower, and improved balance. One way to assist this process is to concentrate on gaining a sense of gently growing taller. Imagine that you are being pulled up from the crown of your head by a piece of string. Focusing your eyes on a specific spot can also help—you will notice it is more difficult (although good practice) to find your balance with your eyes closed. When used as a starting position, Tadasana teaches you steadiness in postures that follow.

Stand with your legs, feet, and heels together, big toe joints touching. Kneecaps are drawn up into your thighs (but not locked), so that legs are well extended. Squeeze your legs together to form a strong, supportive pillar for the rest of your body. Lengthen your spinal column further and the back of your neck, keeping your chin parallel to the ground. Press your abdomen, particularly your lower abdomen, into your spine, raising your diaphragm up under your lower ribs to enhance the lengthening of your lower and middle back (lumbar spine).

Breathe into your chest area, expanding the front and back of your rib cage. Then, as you exhale, press your abdomen closer in toward your spine. Pull down your shoulders, reaching downward through your arms, hands, and fingers, which are held in at your sides. Keep chest and shoulders open. Feel the lengthening up through your central column and the downward extension through the arms and fingers.

As by learning the alphabet one can, through practice, master all the sciences, so by thoroughly practicing first physical training, one acquires the knowledge of Truth ...

—the sage Gheranda

Basic sitting position

Follow instructions as for the standing position in terms of the area from head to hips. In the first two basic sitting positions below, arms hang loosely from your shoulders with the arms placed on your thighs or knees, depending on the position of your legs.

Options for leg positions

(a) From a kneeling position, sit on your heels

(b) Sit cross-legged on a cushion

(Back is straight as hips are slightly above the knees.)

a

b

Dandasana
the Staff Pose
danda = staff, stick

Dandasana can be used as a starting position for sitting forward bends, such as Pascimottanasana, Janu Sirsasana, and Upavista Konasana, as well as a posture in its own right.

Sit with legs together, parallel, and outstretched in front of you with feet flexed, toes pointing upward and heels reaching forward to enhance your leg extension. Kneecaps are pulled into your upper thighs. Your torso is held perpendicular to your legs, and the spine is lengthened. Your navel is pressed gently toward the spine so that you breathe into your chest area and upper abdomen. Head and neck are held in line with your spine, eyes looking forward. Shoulders are relaxed, chest open. Arms are placed in at your sides with hands resting on the ground and fingers pointing forward, in line with your legs.

BREATHING

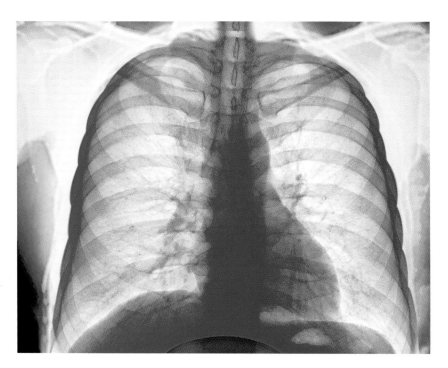

Not only are we dependent upon breathing, the ever-alternating movement between inhalation and exhalation, for life, but the breath is also directly related to our sense of vitality. Our breathing habits and patterns either enhance or deplete our energy reserves.

Breathing patterns are intrinsically linked with our emotions and the state of our mind. For example, it is not possible to feel anxious when breathing in a calm, controlled manner. On the other hand, it is not possible to feel calm when breathing is jerky, hurried, and uneven. The effects of emotional upheaval can be reduced by consciously bringing the breath under control. At any point you can apply the mind to breathing more evenly, calmly, and deeply.

Yoga is a system of exercise that incorporates breathing as a fundamental part of its practice. Conscious and controlled breathing is coordinated with the movement and holding of the physical postures, but breathing is also a practice in its own right. Working with the breath in such a conscious manner assists the flow of movement and serves to focus your attention in the present moment and on the physical task of the pose.

Yoga practice focusing purely on breathing techniques is referred to as Pranayama—"prana" means energy, or life-force, referring to the life-force that animates all forms of life in the universe. Prana, absorbed through the breath, permeates every cell in the human body and is the force behind the renewal and revitalizing of the cells. Thus health and vitality are dependent upon the amount of prana that infuses the body. "Yama" means to lengthen. Pranayama therefore refers to the art of lengthening the breath, and through the breath, enhancing the life-force and energy within us.

Pranayama has the effect of calming the nervous system, focusing and quieting the mind, and cultivating a feeling of serenity within. Thus Pranayama practice assists and

Above   **Yogic breathing, contrary to normal breathing, focuses on increasing the capacity of the lungs through expansion of the upper abdomen and rib cage on inhalation, then engaging the abdominal muscles on exhalation to empty the lungs more fully. Feel the difference by lying on your back with hands folded over the lower abdomen.**

enhances both the practice of Yoga postures and meditation. Bear in mind that, where breathing more fully and efficiently does increase the amount of prana in the body, this does not mean that deeper breathing is always better. There are instances, too, where hyperventilation occurs from breathing too quickly. The aim of Pranayama and other Yoga breathing in general is to enhance the awareness of, and conscious control over, the breath.

Instructions for breathing while doing Yoga postures

- Breathing is always through the nose with the lips gently closed, unless otherwise specified. The nose contains little hairs that filter, warm, and moisten the air before it enters the lungs.
- Each breath is to be slow, deep, and evenly timed on inhalation and exhalation.
- Lengthening the exhalation slightly more than the inhalation (if not contraindicated) promotes relaxation and is used particularly in Pranayama exercises.
- Breathing is to be coordinated with the movement into and out of postures, or between postures.
- While holding a posture, breathing is used as a way to mark the time spent in that posture, for example, to the count of six breaths.
- On doing a Yoga sequence, like the Sun Salutation, you can speed up the breath if you wish to execute the sequence at a faster pace, so long as the breath remains coordinated with movement from one posture to the next. For correct breathing to occur, a healthy posture is required, as this allows an unrestricted flow of the breath and the potential to exercise the diaphragm to its maximum. In full deep breathing, the raising and lowering of the diaphragm exerts a strong pumping action on the lymphatic system, which has a detoxifying effect on the body and aids the functioning of the immune system (lymph nodes neutralize and filter out harmful organisms that are excreted via the kidneys).

To exercise your diaphragm to its maximum, start by breathing into your upper abdominal area and rib cage, feeling the expansion to the front and back of your rib cage. This enlarging of the lung cavity allows more air to be taken into the lungs themselves.

On exhalation, relax your rib cage to allow the breath to flow out. Then toward the end of the exhalation, activate your abdominal muscles. This contraction of the muscles causes the diaphragm to press upward and compress the lungs, helping to expel a greater amount of air.

. . . the consciousness becomes favorably disposed, serene and benevolent . . . by maintaining the pensive state felt at the time of soft and steady exhalation and during passive retention after exhalation.

—Yoga Sutras of Patañjali

PRANAYAMA

the art of breath control

prana = breath, life (universal energy); ayama = expansion, stretching, or restraint (extension and control of the breath)

- For all breathing techniques, aim to do between six and 20 rounds (one round is made up of one inhalation and one exhalation).
- Unless otherwise specified, sit in a comfortable position or lie down in Savasana (see p26).
- Choose one to three techniques per session.

Sectional breathing

This technique helps increase lung capacity by encouraging fuller breathing into the lungs. It has a deeply calming effect on body and mind. Use sectional breathing as an introduction to the Full Yogic Breath.

Breathing into the lower region of the lung

Place your fingers on either side of your navel, with elbows resting on the floor at your sides. Take three breaths into this area and feel your abdomen rising and falling beneath your hands.

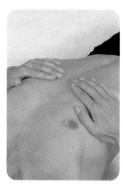

Breathing into the middle region of the lung

Place your hands on each side of your rib cage. Take three breaths, feeling your rib cage expanding sideways under your hands as you inhale and relaxing as you exhale.

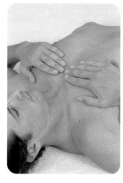

Breathing into the upper region of the lung

Place your fingers underneath your collarbones. As you inhale, feel your upper chest rising slightly. Keep your shoulders relaxed; avoid raising or tensing them.

The full Yogic breath

Place your arms at your sides, palms facing up or down. In a single inhalation, draw air into your lower abdomen, then into your rib cage and finally into the top of your chest. On exhalation, relax as the air flows out.

Left Yoga breathing exercises can be effectively combined with a relaxation pose such as Savasana.

Ujjayi breath

ud = expanding
jayi = conquering, subduing

This soothing technique can be applied to Sectional Breathing or used while holding Yoga postures. It helps increase lung capacity (and more oxygen is absorbed into the bloodstream), energy levels, and also achieves a state of calmness and mental clarity.

Partially close the back of your throat—the epiglottis, which covers the windpipe—so that as you inhale and exhale through your nose, the air passes through a narrower air passage in your throat, creating the sound made by your breathing while you are in a state of deep sleep.

This sound can be likened to the whispering of the letters "hhhhh" expressed on inhalation and exhalation.

Brahmari

the bee breath
Brahmara = bee
(the breath hums like a bee)

Brahmari helps to clear and strengthen the respiratory system and improve vocal resonance. It has a calming effect on the body, uplifts the spirit, and clears and invigorates the mind.

Keeping your lips gently closed throughout, inhale deeply, then hum as you exhale, extending the exhalation as long as possible. Use your abdominal muscles to help control the evenness of your breath on exhalation. Repeat this once more.

If you wish to stimulate your lung cells to further invigorate the vocal resonance and your body, tap your chest with your fists or fingertips as you hum on the outbreath.

If a lengthened exhalation is contraindicated for you, keep inhalations and exhalations even.

Sitali and Sitkari

the cooling breaths

These two techniques have a cooling effect on the body—which is useful during the hot months of the year. They also calm the nervous system. Sitali, particularly, can alleviate nausea and the symptoms of asthma.

Sitali

On inhalation, curl your tongue so that the sides fold up, forming a tube, with your tongue protruding from your lips. Raise your chin as you inhale through your tongue (like a straw), feeling the cool air over the tongue. On exhalation, slightly lower your chin, place the tip of your tongue behind your front teeth, close your lips, and exhale through your nose.

Sitkari

Part your jaw slightly, so that your upper and lower teeth are a small distance apart. Your tongue rests at the base of your mouth, and the corners of your mouth are opened out as if in a wide smile.

Inhale and exhale through your teeth, with the air passing over your tongue. The air should feel cool as it moves over the surface of your tongue during inhalation.

If you are unable to curl your tongue, practice Sitkari instead.

SIMHASANA
the Lion
Simha = Lion

This technique gives the face and arms a good stretch and can relieve a sore throat and other respiratory ailments.

Sit on your haunches, back upright and hands resting on the thighs. Inhale deeply, then exhale with your mouth opened wide, tongue extending out, and eyes looking up to a point between your brows while stretching your arms and spreading and extending your fingers out over your knees. Hold this position while inhaling and exhaling two to five times, and feel the breath in the back of your throat. Then exhale as you return to the starting position.

ANULOMA VILOMA
anuloma = with the natural order
viloma = going against

This technique helps to balance and harmonize the functioning of the right and left hemispheres of the brain. It has a soothing effect on the nervous system and calms the mind. Because exhalations are longer than inhalations, it encourages the removal of stale air and toxins.

Raise your right hand, curling your forefinger and middle finger into your palm, leaving thumb, fourth finger, and little finger extended (1). Place your thumb on the right side of your nose and apply gentle pressure just under the bone, where the fleshy part of the nose begins. Inhale through the left nostril (2). Release and exhale through both nostrils.

Then, using your fourth finger, apply pressure to the left nostril, inhaling through the right (3). Release and exhale through both nostrils. Repeat steps 2 and 3.

General cautions and contra-indications for Pranayama

- It is essential that breathing techniques are first learned under the supervision of an experienced teacher.
- If you feel any kind of discomfort or symptom such as dizziness or nausea arising as you practice breathing, lie down and relax in Savasana or the Child's Pose for a few recovery breaths. If discomfort persists, do not continue your practice until you get advice regarding your symptoms.
- Simple breathing techniques can be used at the start of a session to help calm and focus the mind and body. The practice of Pranayama is highly recommended before relaxation and meditation at the end of a session.

RELAXATION POSTURES

Relaxation practice can be seen as a way to harness the inherent potential of muscles and nerves, since the greatest power in efficient and effective movement is when the ability to relax is also present. This coupled with meditation practice (which trains the mind to be calm and have an unwavering focus), and a stretch and strengthening program such as Hatha Yoga practice (which tones the physical body), can free the power of human potential.

A certain amount of tension is necessary in order to maintain the uprightness of the body. But a certain amount of relaxation is also necessary to create flow in our movement and functioning. Most people have experienced accumulated muscular tension in response to stress, where the muscles are unable to return to a balanced resting state. The result is that too much effort is required to carry out any action, however simple. These tensions eventually become accepted by the body, and we unwittingly carry ourselves in this state every day. The

overall effects of such tension may include reduced energy levels, less flexibility, restriction of the free flow of the breath, and reduced efficiency in your activity. Tension also results in increased vulnerability to injury, sickness, fatigue, or sleep problems. The process of letting go of excess muscular tension is often gradual, especially when this tension has accumulated over many years.

Yoga takes this into account and incorporates relaxation postures as an integral part of the practice. The resulting relaxation also cultivates a state of calmness that naturally filters through into everyday life.

During Yoga practice, the relaxation or rest postures allow the body to absorb and integrate the energy released through the various postures. Time is allowed for the blood to circulate throughout the body after the holding of Yoga positions that concentrate the blood flow in specific areas of the body. This also allows you to gain the full benefit of each posture. Relaxation poses can be incorporated before, during, and after the Yoga session. All the rest poses presented here are symmetrical, and thus help to restore a state of balance to the body. Each position should be held for three to eight breaths or longer.

Left This rest pose is very beneficial to your vital organs, as it encourages the blood to pool in the sacral and lumbar area, nourishing those organs.

Savasana

the Corpse Pose

sava = corpse

This pose is particularly recommended for the final relaxation at the end of a session.

Lie on your back with legs extended and slightly apart; the feet should fall naturally to either side, completely relaxed. Legs are relaxed, too. Arms rest at a 45-degree angle to your torso, with the palms of your hands facing up. The back of the neck is extended, chin slightly tucked in toward the chest, lengthening the upper spine. Take care that the spine and legs are aligned and that you are evenly relaxed on the right and left sides. If this pose is done at the end of a session, remain in Savasana for about five minutes, breathing easily. To come out of the position without disturbing your peaceful state, stretch out your body and take a deep breath.

Roll onto your side into the fetal position, then gradually ease your way up to a sitting or standing position, moving slowly without any sudden or jerky movements.

Supta Vajrasana

the Child's Pose

supta = lying down or resting; va = move ra = radiant (a position that radiates the blood supply to the upper body)

This pose is a forward bend of the torso and relaxes the entire spinal column.

Sit on your haunches, with the arms relaxed at your sides. Bend forward, placing your forehead on the floor, and rest your arms alongside your body with fingers stretched out next to your feet. Shoulders are relaxed over your knees.

An alternate position is to place one fist on top of the other and rest your forehead on both fists.

This version is advised if you have high blood pressure, a heart condition, or any eye problem in which your head should remain above the level of your heart.

If you are pregnant, spread your knees apart in this position to accommodate your abdomen.

Apanasana

the Wind–Relieving Position

apana = subtle energy that moves in abdominal area and controls elimination of waste products from the body

This position gives a wonderful massage to the lower back, as the spine is in contact with the floor throughout and helps relieve tension in this area. The pose also gives a gentle massage to the abdominal organs, thus aiding digestion and relieving wind or gas.

Apanasana can be used as a soothing counterposture to back bends and spinal twists. It is a posture in its own right, too, and can be executed dynamically or statically.

Lie on your back with your body straight and chin slightly tucked in so that the back of the neck is extended. Keep your lower spine, all the way down to your coccyx, in contact with the ground. Bend both legs, hugging your knees over your abdomen with elbows out to the sides.

Hold your knees over your abdomen. Inhaling, raise your knees and move them, hands on knees, as far away from you as your arms will allow. Exhaling, ease your knees back in over your abdomen. Repeat three to eight times, feeling the massage to the lower back.

An alternative position for the legs, working more on mobility and flexibility in the hip joint, is to spread your knees apart keeping the toes touching. Do this version if you are pregnant.

Other options for rest poses

Place a folded blanket/s against a wall and sit on it with one hip against the wall. As you lean back, swivel hips and buttocks, using your hands to help you, to rest against the wall. Then lie on your back while extending legs vertically up the wall. Extend your arms along the floor, reaching out beyond your head.

This version offers a wonderful relaxation for your legs after a Yoga session, particularly when standing postures are included. It is also beneficial for leg problems, such as varicose veins.

Enhance the expansion of your chest, and deepen your breathing into this area in a relaxed pose, by lying over a cushion with your arms extended out to the sides. Place the cushion under the lower or higher section of your rib cage, whichever feels more comfortable.

You can also place the cushion under your hips and lower back area to draw awareness to belly breathing, and breathe into your hip area while giving a passive opening stretch to your hip flexors. This can be helpful when preparing for back-bending postures.

Note: Lie in Savasana for several breaths afterwards as a counterposture to the passive back bend.

STILLING THE MIND

A basic premise in Yoga is that a healthy state of awareness is achieved by an ability to focus and maintain one's attention on the present moment in a calm and clear manner. Meditation is a method of attaining this focus, through the application of specific techniques. It involves the act of quiet contemplation or reflection on the inner self, the nature of the mind, or on something greater than the self—whether this is viewed as God, universal consciousness, or any chosen symbol of divinity. Although meditation is often associated with certain religious paths or rituals, in this book the term is used to describe an ancient practice used to quiet the mind and work toward greater self-knowledge, self-mastery, and a heightened state of awareness. The techniques offered in this book do not promote any particular religion.

To gain the maximum benefit from your Yoga, it is important to practice both the physical postures and meditation. Traditionally, Hatha Yoga is viewed as a preparation for meditation, since the postures, breathing, and relaxation relieve the body of excess tension and calm the nervous system, resulting in reduced restlessness when sitting still for meditation. The postures and breathing also focus the mind and train you to maintain this focus in the present moment— meditation's ultimate goal. Practising meditation regularly, in turn, is helpful to your Hatha Yoga, as the nervous

system is calmed, and the resultant state of serenity assists the practice of postures. Areas of tension that could hinder your practice are identified and released and you learn to gain greater control over your mind's chatter, which can be distracting to your Yoga and your ability to truly relax.

MEDITATION TECHNIQUES

A meditative state can be achieved in many different ways, for example, focusing on an object, image, or even a word or phrase. Be aware that in the beginning, meditation will not be about how long you can maintain a state of mental clarity and focus. Rather, it is about developing an ability to return your attention to a selected point of focus time and time again. It is inevitable that your mind will wander, with thoughts and emotions arising endlessly, drawing you into their content and distracting your focus. As soon as you notice that your mind has wandered, simply return your attention to your chosen focal point. As you learn to allow thoughts and emotions to arise and pass, they will eventually have less and less power to distract your attention. Try not to become frustrated with yourself when your mind wanders; simply redirect your attention to the clarity of the present moment.

Above Buddhists are well versed in the art of **meditation. With regular practice, it** *does* **become easier over time.**

- In general (except for the Full Lotus position) it is advisable to sit on a cushion or folded blanket so that your hips are slightly raised above the level of your knees. This promotes a straight spine.
- You may want to place your cushion on a soft surface, like a carpet, mat, or blanket, so that your knees and feet are also comfortable.
- Sit relaxed, but with your spine extending upward right to the back of your neck by slightly lowering your chin toward your chest.
- Make sure you are well settled in this position, feeling the strength of your straight back and the softness of the front of your body.
- Breathing is full, on each inhalation expanding gently into the abdomen, the rib cage, and upper chest sequentially. On exhalation this process is reversed, so that the abdomen is the last to exhale fully as it presses gently toward the spine to assist more complete exhalation.
- Lips are gently sealed, with the tip of your tongue placed on your palate behind your front teeth, allowing your jaw to relax.
- If the eyes are open, rest them in a relaxed manner on your chosen focal point.
- Start with five or 10 minutes' meditation to gradually build up your stamina for stillness. Build up to 20 minutes. Work toward sitting for 20 or 30 minutes a day, or 45 minutes at least three times a week.

When the senses are stilled, when the mind is at rest, when the intellect wavers not . . . this steady control of the senses and mind has been defined as Yoga.

—Kathopanishad (the Upanishads)

SEATED POSES

SUKHASANA

sukha = happy, easy, comfortable

Sukhasana is a "comfortable" or "easy" sitting position. You can adapt this to suit your needs; by sitting on a cushion with your legs crossed; or if you have knee problems, sitting with one or both legs extended out in front of you.

SIDDHASANA

Siddha = a sage / prophet

Start in Sukhasana with legs crossed. Take hold of one ankle or foot, place it on top of the other leg, with the outer edge of the raised foot pressing into the opposite calf, thigh, or groin. If you use this position regularly, make sure you alternate the leg that is raised so you develop flexibility evenly in both legs and hips.

PADMASANA

the Lotus Position

padma = lotus

Start in Sukhasana, move into Siddhasana, then lift the other leg, pressing the outer edge of the foot into the opposite groin. Take hold of both feet and ease them further in toward your groin, aiming for a balanced, symmetrical position.

Options for hand positions (Mudras)

The hand positions are designed to help center the energy in your body by creating a closed circuit in which it can circulate. Start by placing the hands palms down on knees or thighs, with the arms and elbows resting at your sides and shoulders relaxed.

a

a) Hands rest with the palms facing down on thighs or knees.

b) Palms face up, and the tips of the forefinger and thumb touch, forming a closed circle. This is known as the Chin Mudra position.

b

c) Cradle your left hand in your right, palms up and thumbs touching above the center of the palm.

c

Meditation techniques

Two meditation techniques are offered here, to assist the mind to focus on the present moment. If you have learned of another technique in a Yoga class or at a meditation center, feel free to apply the one that you find most effective.

Focus on the breath

Focus your attention by simply observing the natural flow of your breath without changing it in any way. You can also focus your attention on each exhalation, allowing tensions and emotions to be relaxed with each out-breath. Particularly notice the pause between the end of the exhalation and the start of the inhalation. Eyes can be open or closed. If your eyes are open, rest them on the floor a few feet away from your body, so that your eyes are gently downcast, focusing not too far from your body.

Above and right When using an object in meditation, the idea is not to scrutinize its detail, but rather to use it as a neutral focal point to which your eyes can return whenever you are aware of your attention having strayed.

Left Being in a serenely beautiful environment is very inspiring for meditation, particularly if you are a beginner.

Focus on an object

Place a lighted candle on the floor a few feet away from you or on a surface at eye level. Place your attention on the candle; your aim is to focus on the flame. Whenever your mind wanders, bring it gently back to the flame. You can also close your eyes and focus on the lingering image of the flame in your mind until it fades, then open the eyes and look at it again.

This technique offers a way for a couple or whole family to meditate together, as members can sit in a circle and focus on the same candle flame.

You can replace the candle with a beautiful object, such as a flower or a textured stone. The object should be as simple in shape or design as possible, so that the mind is not distracted by intricate decoration. Again, its main purpose is to refocus your attention when it wanders.

YOUR *Yoga practice at home should complement your learning Yoga from a teacher. The guidance and supervision that an experienced teacher will give you when you join a Yoga class is an essential addition to your learning of Yoga from this book.*

When you practice on your own, it is important to work within your personal physical (and realistic) limits, and be gentle with yourself. If you repeatedly feel drained and exhausted after Yoga practice, then you may be pushing yourself too hard. Be mindful of your attitude toward yourself and your approach to your practice.

Yoga at Home

PREPARATION FOR YOGA AT HOME

A PLACE TO PRACTICE

Yoga can be practiced inside or outside your home, but certain factors need to be taken into account. Choose a clear, open space that is large enough for you to extend your limbs while standing and lying down; move furniture if necessary. The space should be as clean and quiet as possible, and the surface on which you practice needs to be firm and level.

If the space is inside, the room temperature should be moderate. If you are outside, be mindful of the sun or extreme weather conditions.

WHEN TO PRACTICE

Consistency encourages discipline and yields the greatest rewards, so set aside a regular time. Experiment to decide what time of day you prefer. Morning practice sets the tone for the day ahead, preparing your mind and body and loosening up stiff muscles. Evening practice facilitates unwinding and releasing of the day's stress and tension.

PERSONAL PREPARATION

• Select comfortable, loose-fitting clothing or elasticized gym gear that allows you freedom of movement. Avoid wearing clothing that restricts your breathing or blood circulation.

• Keep the feet bare, unless it is very cold; you may wear socks until you warm up.

• Where this is practical, remove any jewelry.

Above and right **Before beginning with Yoga postures, allow a time span of three to four hours after eating a heavy meal, and one to two hours after a light meal or a snack. Fluids should not be drunk directly before the session.**

LENGTH OF YOUR PRACTICE

Generally, a session can last from 15 minutes to two hours. Allow sufficient time for postures, relaxation, breathing practices, and meditation—never rush your practice. An hour or an hour and a half is an ideal amount of time. If the time you have is limited, choose fewer postures to focus on and perhaps set aside a separate time to meditate, such as first thing in the morning or before bed at night. Ideas for different-length sessions are offered in Chapter 6.

YOGA PROPS

Practice on a nonslip surface to help you hold the postures steadily. Use a Yoga mat or a suitable substitute such as a rubber camping mat. A layered blanket or towel/s can also be used, particularly outdoors. The following list of props is optional, but can be helpful to your practice.

- Cushions
- A strap (around 2m, or 6ft, long) or belt
- A block
- A blanket
- A chair
- A full-length mirror (this is useful for assisting you in checking your alignment).

GENERAL SAFETY PRECAUTIONS

- Read all Yoga instructions carefully.
- Never force any posture to a point where it produces pain. By pushing yourself too hard, you can strain or sprain a muscle or ligament. It is important to discern the difference between constructive stretching and pain when you push your body too far.
- Aim to remain as aware as possible of your breathing and body sensation while executing postures, as this teaches you to remain focused and mindful throughout your Yoga session.
- Never attempt a more difficult version of a posture until you can comfortably execute the simpler version and can hold it for at least six deep breaths.
- If you have a chronic medical condition, such as asthma, diabetes, or heart disease, keep your medication with you while practicing.

DEVISING A YOGA SESSION

It is important to learn to respect and listen to the innate intelligence of your body. A helpful suggestion is to pay attention to how you are feeling each day and adjust your Yoga practice accordingly.

A sample 30-minute Yoga session		
Rest poses	*Apanasana*	*p27*
Neutral	*Leg Raises*	*p50*
Back bend (dynamic)	*Bidalasana*	*p55*
Neutral	*Chaturangsana*	*p81*
Back bend	*Adho Mukha Svanasana*	*p56*
Forward bend	*Supta Vajrasana*	*p26*
Forward bend	*Pascimottanasana*	*p51*
Forward bend (balance)	*Paripurna Navasana*	*p52*
Neutral	*Savasana*	*p26*
Back bend	*Bhujangasana*	*p58*
Forward bend	*Supta Vajrasana*	*p26*
Brahmari in Savasana		
Meditation		

POSTURE GROUPS AND THE POSTURE SUMMARY CHART

All postures in this book have been categorized into one of six groups: sitting forward bends, sitting back bends, standing postures, balancing postures (standing and on the hands), inverted postures, and rest postures.

On the Posture Summary Chart on p39, these posture groups have been further categorized in accordance with the orientation of each posture:

- neutral—the spine is in a vertical or horizontal orientation in space, or where upper and lower body form a straight line in its vertical or horizontal orientation
- forward bend
- back bend
- side bend
- twist.

These categories are aimed at assisting you in choosing complementary postures for each session. For example, working with sitting forward bends goes well with standing forward bend/s later in the session, and working with back bends can prepare you for a balancing posture that incorporates a back bend such as one of the Natarajasana (the Dancer) poses. Breathing and meditation practices are not included on the chart.

For easy reference, only one version of each posture is depicted on the chart—detailed instructions are presented in Chapters 4 and 5. Once you have selected your postures, turn to the relevant pages for the photographed sequence and accompanying instructions to practice the version that is suitable for your level of flexibility and strength.

WARMING UP THROUGH SIMPLIFIED POSTURES

Take care to first warm up the relevant areas of your body in preparation for a safe execution of the postures you have selected to work with.

Warm-up suggestions are offered on the same page as the detailed postures. Don't be discouraged if, as a beginner, you find that you are capable of executing only the warm-up exercises. If this is the case, work at the level you are comfortable with, using this as a gauge to progress to more advanced versions over time.

MOVING FROM SIMPLE TO MORE CHALLENGING

These may include postures from different groups or may focus on a particular posture group. For a simple, short session select between two and six postures. It is advisable to work slowly from the neutral version of a posture, moving gradually toward the fuller respective posture.

It is also good to use forward bends at the start of a session, before moving on to other posture groups. Postures used in the beginning of the session should prepare you for more challenging versions later in the session.

POSTURES AND COUNTERPOSTURES

Every posture needs to be balanced by a counteracting posture that either bends the body in the opposite direction or returns the body to a position of symmetry. In this way, the body gains full benefit from the postures. If you experience discomfort after doing a posture, you can remedy the problem with a counterposture (below), whether it be an active or a rest pose. Always recuperate in a rest pose after a challenging posture or a series of postures.

COUNTERPOSTURES

- A counterposture should be easier than a preceding posture and can take the form of a rest pose.
- Hold the counterposture for at least a third of the time that you held the preceding posture or final static pose of a sequence.
- Postures must be alternated with counterpostures throughout the session. You can do two or three postures of the same group before doing a counterposture, e.g. for, say, back bends, warm up with the dynamic version of Bhujangasana (Cobra), move into the static version, followed by a forward bend. Or use Setu Bandha Sarvangasana (Little Bridge), followed by Sarvangasana and Halasana (Plow), before moving into Matsyasana (Fish) as a counterposture.
- Follow all back bends with a forward bend.
- Spinal twists and side bends need to be preceded and followed by a symmetrical posture in a forward bend—never a back bend.
- After carrying out a twist or a side bend on one side of the body, return to a symmetrical position before twisting or bending the other way. This returns the spine to its correct alignment as a starting point for bending in the opposite direction.
- Inverted postures should be followed by a rest pose such as Supta Vajrasana (Child's Pose) or Savasana (Corpse Pose). This allows the blood flow to return to normal in the body. Do not stand up too quickly after an inverted posture, as this may cause dizziness.

Note

Breathing is particularly advised before relaxation and meditation practice, although it can also be included at any stage in a session.

BALANCE POSTURES

Choose a balance that works on the area of your body that has warmed up. For example, if you have included Baddha Konasana (Butterfly Pose) in your session, you will find Vrksasana (Tree Pose) easier to achieve. If you focus on forward bends, you could balance in Paripurna Navasana or Utthita Hasta Padangusthasana.

Include balances toward the end of your session, when your mind and body are well prepared.

REST POSTURES

Rest postures should be included at least three or four times during a session to allow your body to relax between postures. You can also begin a session with a rest posture to prepare mind and body, so that you take a relaxed approach to the session. Each session needs to conclude with a rest pose, such as Savasana (the Corpse Pose). Stay in this position for five to 10 minutes.

MEDITATION

Where possible, meditation is advised at the end of a session, otherwise at a separate time of day. A good, simple meditation to begin with is one that uses the breath as a point on which to focus. As soon as your mind wanders, gently bring it back to concentrate on your breathing.

First, become an observer, and in your mind's eye watch the passage of the breath entering and leaving the nose. Feel it move in and out of your nostrils. Once you sense a feeling of quiet, you can then follow the breath's course into your lungs and out again. Relax into its modulated rhythm and experience the feeling of peace that fills your body.

I bow before the noblest of sages, Patañjali, who brought serenity of mind by his work on Yoga, clarity of speech by his work on grammar and purity of body by his work on medicine.

—A Yoga Prayer

POSTURE SUMMARY CHART

SITTING or LYING

Neutral
- Dandasana p19
- Vajrasana p46
- Supta Vajrasana p46
- Gomukhasana p47

Forward Bend
- Baddha Konasana p48
- Supta Baddha Konasana p49
- Upavista Konasana p49
- Janu Sirshasana p50
- Pascimottanasana p51
- Paripurna Navasana p52

- Bidalasana p55

Back Bend
- Downward-facing Dog p56
- Chandrasana p57
- Bhujangasana p58
- Matsyasana p59
- Setu Bandha Sarvangasana p60
- Purvottanasana p81

Side bend
- Jathara Parivartanasana p63
- Ardha Matsyendrasana p65

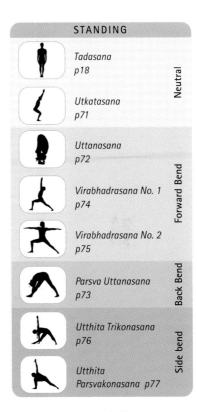

STANDING

Neutral
- Tadasana p18
- Utkatasana p71

Forward Bend
- Uttanasana p72
- Virabhadrasana No. 1 p74
- Virabhadrasana No. 2 p75

Back Bend
- Parsva Uttanasana p73

Side bend
- Utthita Trikonasana p76
- Utthita Parsvakonasana p77

STANDING BALANCE

Neutral
- Utthita Hasta Padangusthasana p79
- Natarajasana p79

Back Bend
- Vrksasana p80

HAND BALANCE

Neutral
- Chaturangsana p81

Back Bend
- Purvottanasana p81

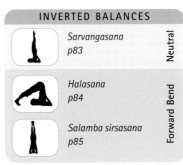

INVERTED BALANCES

Neutral
- Sarvangasana p83

Forward Bend
- Halasana p84
- Salamba sirsasana p85

REST POSES

Neutral
- Savasana p26

Forward Bend
- Supta Vajrasana p26
- Apanasana p27

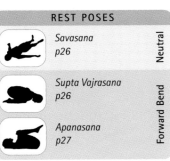

COUNTERPOSTURES

Neutral
- Tadasana p18

Forward Bend
- Against a wall p27
- Hanging forward bend p69

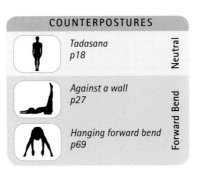

THE word "asana" appears at the end of each Sanskrit name for the Yoga postures, and refers to a pose assumed by the physical body in a comfortable and steady manner.

Physically, the asanas tone and strengthen, while cultivating poise and flexibility. They work to free the body of tensions accumulated in our daily existence and strengthen the functioning of the body's various systems. Thus we experience the sense of vitality and joy that Yoga practitioners associate with accessing the true nature of the soul—the inherent potential of all human beings. On an emotional and mental level, a state of calmness and clarity is cultivated. On a spiritual level asanas work to free up communication blocks in the subtle body through the subtle energy centers (such as the chakras) associated with the endocrine and central nervous systems, both of which influence the immune system. These systems are brought into a state of balance.

Sitting Postures

WHERE TO BEGIN

The manner in which you assume Yoga postures is important. Be gentle and caring with yourself and your approach to your practice. Assuming postures with frowned seriousness or tension-filled effort can reduce the effectiveness of Yoga and can even lead to injury. Keep in mind that even a hint of a smile on your face relieves facial tension, which can have a relaxing influence on the level of tension in your entire body. It is important to find enjoyment in your practice; you in turn increase levels of flexibility, strength, and range of motion, and move toward a heightened sense of body and mind awareness.

This chapter includes Western posture variations and simplifications that are widely taught and recognized in Yoga classes. They serve as ways to introduce postures to the beginner, who may not have the flexibility, strength, or mental focus required to execute a posture in its classical form. Postures are divided into the following groups: sitting postures (including forward bends, back bends, and spinal twists), standing postures, balances (including standing and hand balances), inverted postures, and rest postures.

General notes on posture execution

- Read instructions carefully and always begin with the simplest version of the posture, moving progressively through each instruction.
- Only do the versions you can hold without straining for the suggested length of time. You will find that you improve over time, with regular practice, and will be able to progress onto more advanced levels.
- You do not need to achieve the most advanced version of a posture in order to gain the benefits. By staying true to the level you have reached, and maintaining your practice at this level, the maximum benefit will be attained.
- Do not feel disheartened or inferior if physical restrictions such as muscular tightness, limitations in joint mobility, or old injuries prevent your body from attaining some of the more advanced posture versions. Be assured that you are gaining the benefits at your level of ability.
- Approach postures mindfully and with care, making sure that you do not bounce or force your body into any posture.

Above **Here, lines of perfect symmetry reflect the mental and physical poise that Yoga sets out to achieve.**

Opposite **Although some balancing poses appear to require great strength, they rely more on accomplishing a perfect state of equilibrium between opposite sides of the body.**

Dynamic versus static version of postures

Dynamic posture execution refers to moving into and out of a posture repeatedly and with care, coordinating breath with movement. Dynamic postures focus the mind, while encouraging deeper breathing. The body also becomes accustomed to the motion required to move into and out of postures, and those areas that are to be involved in subsequent postures are warmed up—so where dynamic versions are recommended, they may be used in preparation for static postures.

Static posture execution refers to holding a posture for a period of time, which in this book is to be counted in breaths. In Yoga "static" does not mean inactive or passive; it refers to a held state that is vitally alive through conscious breathing and body extension or flexion. Aim to find a state of balance between relaxing into a posture while actively extending out of it—this helps prevent the accumulation of excess tension. Conscious breathing also keeps postures alive.

While holding a static posture, it is useful to scan your body for areas that may be holding tension and perhaps other areas that are not working hard enough to assist in maintaining that posture. For example, you may find your jaw and facial muscles tensing or one side of your body working harder than the other. Aim to balance out whatever inconsistencies you find in a gentle and caring manner. Adding a smile can do wonders in softening a tense attitude.

WARMING UP

This book offers, with every Yoga posture, suggestions for warming up the body and preparing the mind for that posture. It is important to include a warmup in your practice for a number of reasons.

- It helps prepare your body to attain the poses with greater ease, thus helping to prevent injuries. It also helps develop body awareness, which can be applied throughout your Yoga practice (and life).

- It improves blood circulation, which is helpful for sensing body alignment and fuller extension in postures.

- It helps you focus on breathing more fully and evenly. This in turn increases oxygen intake, enhancing energy levels and concentration. To add to this, muscular stiffness from Yoga practice can be reduced if the body is well warmed up beforehand, as the increased blood circulation and oxygen supply to the muscles aid faster removal of toxins and waste products in the muscles.

Forward bends

Forward bends require—thus develop—flexibility in the body. On a physical level, flexibility demands that you learn to surrender or soften into the postures, finding a balance in surrendering or resting in that pose, while also feeling your body extended and actively alive in the pose. On a psychological level, this promotes a calm and self-nurturing quality that can influence the way you move through your life—that is, making you aware of extremes, such as excessive effort or excessive laziness.

On the level of the subtle body, forward bends influence a number of energy centers (chakras), particularly the second energy center (around the navel and lower back area) associated with the kidneys and adrenal glands. Forward bends have a balancing effect on these areas and soothe the nervous system, also calming and quieting the mind.

A relaxed and calm state can be brought about through the activation of the parasympathetic nervous system, which is achieved in the practice of forward bends.

The adrenal glands produce hormones that drive our "fight or flight" response to fear and stimulate our survival instinct. Because of the stresses of modern, competitive, and fast-paced lifestyles, many people spend a greater amount of time than necessary in "fight or flight" mode, which activates the sympathetic nervous system. As a result, people struggle to relax and find mental clarity.

It is worthwhile to note, however, that although fear is regarded as an undesirable emotion, it is a necessary and valuable part of life. Fear invites us to learn and grow through it by facing those fears and cultivating insight, wisdom, and courage. Fear can also be a means of signaling our attention to the possibility of being hurt or our lives being endangered. It is only when fear becomes debilitating that it is detrimental. Even then, it is inviting our attention, and if we persist in reacting in a fearful way, this encourages the accumulation of unnecessary tensions in the body and can hold us back from accepting change and being able to explore and adapt to new situations.

Approach your Yoga postures with this in mind—taking small steps toward achieving postures you may not have thought you were capable of doing. This can help you overcome your fears.

General notes
- If you are a beginner, start with sitting forward bends; this is good preparation before moving on to standing forward bends.
- Forward bends are advised as counterpostures before and after back bends, side bends, and twists.

Benefits
- Extend the spine; promote a healthy spinal column and improve posture.
- Increase flexibility in the hamstrings.
- Activate the parasympathetic nervous system, which has a calming influence.
- Give a gentle squeeze and massage to the abdominal organs, helping to tone them.
- Aid digestion and elimination.

Right We often are not aware of the way bad, or unbalanced, posture affects the spine in daily life. The practice of forward bends, particularly, greatly enhances this awareness and the importance of maintaining a straight spine.

GENERAL PREPARATORY EXERCISES

EYE EXERCISES

These exercises help you to ease any tension in and around the eyes. The resulting relaxed focus should be applied while practicing Yoga.

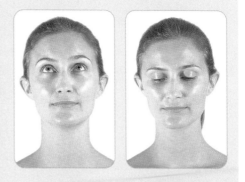

Move eyes up, down, side to side, and diagonally up and down from top corner to opposite bottom corner. Circle eyes two or three times one way, then the other, keeping your eyes focused throughout.

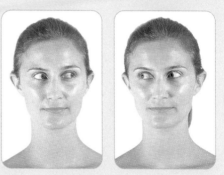

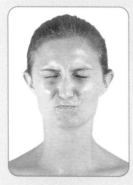

FACIAL MUSCLES

This exercise relieves tension in the jaw.
Alternate the following:
On inhalation, tighten your facial muscles, closing your eyes tightly and pursing your lips. Hold for two or three breaths.

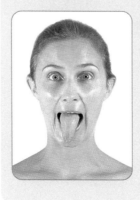

While exhaling, open up your face by opening your eyes and mouth as wide as possible and sticking out your tongue. Hold for two or three breaths.

During your Yoga, keep the front section of your tongue on your palate, tip of the tongue behind the front teeth. Lips are gently sealed. Maintain this (unless otherwise specified).

45

VAJRASANA

the Diamond Pose

vajra = thunderbolt

also, va = to move; ra = radiant
(radiates blood supply and
subtle energies to upper body)

asana = pose

Kneel with legs together, toes pointing out behind you, and sit back on your heels. Big toes (or big toe joints) touch with heels apart, and the spine extends upward. Place your hands palms down on your thighs, head and eyes look straight ahead.

This posture can be held for long periods of time, or for three to six breaths in preparation for Supta Vajrasana (forward bend).

Caution

If you have knee strain, place a cushion or folded blanket in the fold of your legs.

SUPTA VAJRASANA

supta = lying down, resting

Start in Vajrasana. Inhale, stretching up from your waist while extending your arms overhead (1). Exhale, bending forward from your hips, keeping your arms next to your ears until your hands rest on the ground (2). As a dynamic version, inhale while reversing the path taken into the position, allowing your spine to round (3). Repeat three to six times. As a static pose, remain in this position for three to six breaths. Return to Vajrasana with hands resting on the thighs.

Caution

Avoid Vajrasana, Mandukasana, and the leg position in Gomukhasana if you have varicose veins or if your knees feel strained.

MANDUKASANA

the Frog

manduka = frog

Follow the instructions as for Supta Vajrasana, but spread your knees wide apart while keeping your big toes touching. This version helps increase flexibility in the hips and inner thighs. Hold this position as for Vajrasana. This is a good pose if you are pregnant.

GOMUKHASANA

the Cow-face Pose

go = cow; mukha = face

also, go = light; gomukh = light in or of the head (lightness of the head)

Moving into the leg position

Kneel with feet pointing behind you and hands on the ground directly under your shoulders (1). Cross your right leg in front of your left (2), so that your thighs are touching. Sit down between your heels, so that you are sitting upright with spine extended (3). Bring feet in as close to your hips as you can.

1   2   3

Moving into the arm position

Raise your left elbow to point upward, placing your left hand palm down on your back, below the nape of your neck, and centered between the shoulder blades. Use your right hand to take the left elbow as far back behind the head as you can (1), keeping your head upright.

Bend your right elbow and twist your forearm behind your back, so that the back of the hand rests against your spine, palm facing out. Hook both hands together (2), centering them between your shoulder blades; your torso remains symmetrical. Hold for three to eight breaths. Repeat to the other side.

1

2

Options

If you are struggling with flexibility sit on a cushion. Sit cross-legged or in Vajrasana.

COUNTERPOSTURE

Sit in Vajrasana or cross-legged, hook your fingers behind your neck, and gently pull your arms in opposite directions, elbows pointing out horizontally to the sides to give an even stretch across your chest.

Option

Hold a strap between your hands if you cannot bring them together.

PREPARATORY EXERCISES

Lying on your back, bend your legs and place the soles of your feet together with the knees opened out to the sides. Take hold of your ankles or the top of your feet (1) and remain in this position for three to six breaths.

Work toward straightening your legs out to the sides (you can work with them bent if this is your acceptable level), while pressing gently down on your inner thighs (2) or on your feet, depending on where your hands are resting. Hold for three to six breaths.

Sitting upright, place the soles of your feet together with your knees opened out to the sides. Take hold of your ankles or feet. Gently bounce your knees up and down for a minute.

BADDHA KONASANA

the Butterfly

baddha = bound; kona = angle

Sit upright with the soles of the feet together, knees bent and opened out to the sides. The spine is extended upward through to the head. Draw your feet in as close to your body as you can maintain, taking hold of your feet or ankles to help you achieve the position.

Options

To help maintain an extended spine, sit on a cushion.

You can use a wall to help you assume this pose. Face the wall, using it to support the positioning of your legs. Your arms can assist you in keeping your back straight.

SUPTA BADDHA KONASANA

Start in Baddha Konasana, inhale, and imagine you are growing taller through your spine and head (1).

On an exhalation, lean forward from your hips, initiating the movement from the lower part of your spine, while keeping the spine extended and head and neck in line with the spine (2). Open your chest area.

Still holding your feet or ankles, use them as a leverage to help you bend forward further. Extend your elbows out to the sides and keep pressing your knees down toward the ground. Open your chest area as you hold the pose.

UPAVISTA KONASANA

the Straddle

upavista = seated; kona = angle

Start in Baddha Konasana, then straighten and widen your legs as much as you can, flexing your feet to encourage the extension of the back of your legs (1). Place your hands on the ground in front of you and inhale, extending your spine upward. On an exhalation, lean forward from the hips, keeping your spine extended, head and neck in line with the spine (2). Walk your hands forward on the ground as far as you are able while maintaining a straight spine (3). Keep your weight evenly distributed on both sides of the body. Recover, starting on an inhalation, and reverse the path taken into the position.

Options
(a) Sit on a cushion
(b) Bend your knees slightly.
Work toward straightening your legs eventually.

Timing for all postures
Hold static postures for four to 12 breaths.

PREPARATORY EXERCISE

Lie on your back, both legs extended on the ground and feet flexed (1). Raise your right leg and take hold of your ankle (2), holding for three to six breaths. Keep your lower back pressed into the ground and both legs straight throughout. Repeat with the left leg.

Then raise both legs simultaneously, flexing both feet and holding this position either with your arms at your sides (3) or using your arms to support your legs, as for the single leg raises.

Use a strap slung around your foot to help you achieve this position.

JANU SIRSASANA

Head to knee pose

janu = knee; sirsa = head

Start in Dandasana. Bend your right leg, opening it out to the side and pressing your knee down toward the ground. Press your right heel into the left inner thigh as close to your groin as possible (1). The left leg remains active. Both hips face squarely forward. Inhaling, raise both arms forward and up alongside your ears, fingers pointing upward (2). Exhaling, bend forward from your hips, keeping the spine ex-tended. Take hold of your left ankle or foot with both hands, keeping your head and neck in line with the rest of your spine (3), or move into the full position with head to knee. For the dynamic version, reverse the pathway taken into the position, starting with an inhalation. Exhale and return your arms down to your side. Repeat three to six times, then move into the static version.

Static version

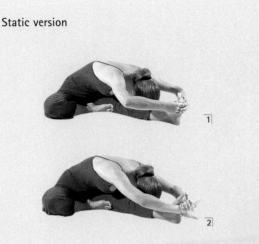

Once you have exhaled into the forward bend, take hold of your left foot (1) or ankle, using both hands for leverage to assist your bend. The left hand can also wrap around the outside of the foot to hold the right wrist (2). Keep your spine, neck, and head extended.

Options

Sit on a cushion to assist the extension of your spine (a); sling a strap around your foot (b); place your hands as far down your leg as you can—knee or ankle (c).

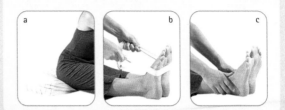

To move into the full position, lower your forehead toward your knee, using your arms to gently assist your forward bend (2). To recover, reverse the path taken into the pose. Repeat the forward bend on your other leg for an equal length of time.

Pascimottanasana

Sitting forward stretch

pascima = back; uttana = extension

Start in Dandasana. Keeping both legs extended throughout and moving both arms simultaneously, follow the instructions as for Janu Sirsasana for both the dynamic and static versions. Take care to work at a level you are comfortable with. To recover, reverse the path taken into the posture.

Timing for all postures
Hold static postures for four to 12 steady breaths.

PREPARATORY EXERCISES

Body curl

Lie on your back, with legs together or apart, toes pointing forward, and arms extended alongside your head (1). Inhale and stretch legs and arms away from your center, keeping them on the floor. Exhale and curl your body into a tight ball, bringing knees to forehead and hugging your legs with your arms (2). Repeat two or three times as a spinal warmup and to strengthen your abdominal muscles.

The rolling ball

This offers a wonderful massage to the spinal column, although it should be avoided if you are not able to round your spine sufficiently, or if you experience any discomfort while attempting it. Start lying on your back. Hug knees into the chest, hands wrapped under your bent knees (1). Round your spine and tuck your chin into your chest, maintaining this position throughout. Initiate a smooth backward and forward rocking motion (2), reaching your legs overhead and swinging them forward to continue the motion. Repeat several times.

PARIPURNA NAVASANA

the Boat

paripurna = complete, full, entire

nava = boat

Sit upright with knees bent and feet flat on the ground. Extend arms parallel to the ground, hands and fingers pointing forward (1). Lean backward from your hips, keeping your spinal column straight, as you extend upward through the head, keeping head and neck in line with the spine. Raise your lower legs so that they are parallel to the ground (2), with feet and toes pointed. Take care that your weight is evenly balanced over both buttocks.

If you are able to maintain the above position for three to six breaths, then extend your legs so that your body forms a "V" shape (3). To assist your balance, reach forward with your arms while extending your spine and legs in a diagonal stretch.

> **Timing**
> Hold for three to eight breaths.

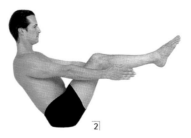

BACK BENDS

Back bends develop strength in the muscles of the back and increase flexibility in the spinal column, which keeps the spine elastic and helps improve posture. Back bends also benefit the nervous system by increasing blood supply to, and therefore nourishing, the spinal area and the nerves that extend out from the spinal column. Improved blood flow to the pelvic area nourishes the reproductive organs.

The abdominal area is stretched and strengthened, assisting digestion, and its organs toned, balancing the functioning of the kidneys and adrenal glands. Finally, back bends expand and open the chest area, improve the flexibility of the shoulders, counter a hunched back and rounded shoulders, and encourage deeper breathing.

On a psychological level, when we worry excessively, dwell on obsessive thoughts, and experience feelings of not being able to progress in life, these emotions are often felt physically as knots of tension in the area between the navel and the rib cage—the region of the solar plexus. The practice of back bends can help work through this by opening and stretching the solar plexus, offering relief to the tension accumulated here. It takes determination and willpower to rise above anxiety, and this in turn can motivate you and influence your attitude to life. On a mental level, while holding a back bend you bring the mind into a state of passive stillness, which leads to improved focus—thus allowing you to cultivate greater will and determination.

On a subtle energetic level, back bends influence a number of energy centers, with particular focus on the solar plexus, throat, and heart energy.

Right **In back bends, it is crucial to balance the flexing of the spinal column in one direction with the relieving counterposture of a forward bend.**

Cautions

- Always use a forward bend directly before and after back bends as a counterposture.
- Never do a spinal twist or side bend directly before or after a back bend.
- Make sure your back and shoulders are well warmed up before you do back bends to avoid any straining of the muscles.
- If you have any back problems, take care to support your back bend by tightening into your buttock muscles to support your lower back (tuck in your tailbone, or coccyx). Also work with dynamic postures to develop greater flexibility and strength in your upper and middle back, such as Bhujangasana (Cobra).
- If you have a neck problem or feel discomfort in this area, do not involve your head and neck in the back bend; instead, keep your head in line with your spine throughout.
- Move slowly and with care when moving into and out of back-bending postures, particularly in relation to your neck.
- If you are pregnant, avoid postures that involve lying on your abdomen and be mindful about how far you take a back bend.

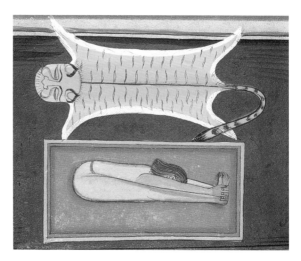

GENERAL PREPARATORY EXERCISES

NECK RELEASES

These exercises help to relax your neck. They should be practiced slowly and with care.

Turning the head

Coordinate your breath in a flowing manner with your movement. You should inhale as you turn your head to one side, then exhale as you return your head to face forward. Aim to keep your chin parallel to the floor throughout. Alternate the movements between two and four times.

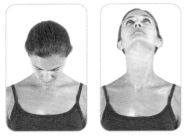

Raising and lowering the head

On an exhalation lower your chin to your chest to stretch the back of your neck. Hold for two to four breaths. On an inhalation return your head to the upright position. Again, on an inhalation, raise your chin, stretching the front of your neck. Exhale, lowering your chin all the way to your chest for one or two breaths. If you have a neck problem, do not try the raising of the chin version.

Stretching the neck

Exhale and lower your ear toward your left shoulder to stretch the right side of the neck. Hold this position for two breaths. Inhale, recovering to the center. Repeat to the other side.

SHOULDER RELEASES

For all of the following exercises, make two or three circles with your shoulders or arms, first forward, then backward. Inhale as your shoulders or arms are raised and exhale as they are lowered. Start by circling your shoulders (1). Then place your hands on your shoulders and circle your elbows (2), keeping shoulders pressed down throughout. Finally straighten your arms (3) and make circles with your arms, also keeping shoulders pressed down throughout.

Above Here, the intense stretch occurring along the side of the waist and rib cage is good for relieving muscular tension.

BIDALASANA

the Cat Stretch

Dynamic version

Start on all fours, with knees hip distance apart and hands under your shoulders (1). Spine is extended in a tabletop position, with head and neck held in line with the rest of your spine, so that eyes look to the ground between your hands.

Inhaling, hollow your back so that your navel lowers toward the ground and your chest expands (2). Keep your shoulder blades pressed down into your back. Exhaling, round your spine, initiating the movement from your navel (3).

Repeat, alternating the hollowing and rounding of your spine four to eight times.

Dynamic version with the legs

Perform as for the version above, including a leg movement as follows:

On inhalation, extend your right leg straight out behind you or higher if you can, your foot pointed or flexed (1). On exhalation, bring your knee in toward your forehead (2). Do two or three times with the right leg. Repeat with the left leg.

Static version in Full Cat Stretch

Start on all fours as for the dynamic version (1), then walk your hands forward (2) until you can place your forehead on the floor in the final pose. Keep your hips raised so that your thighs remain at right angles to the floor. Relax your spine in this position, allowing your lower back area to hang downward from your hips. Hold for three to eight breaths or more. To recover, sit back on your heels and relax with your torso resting on your thighs for a few breaths before returning to all fours.

Caution

Avoid if you have high blood pressure or a heart condition (head is lower than the heart).

COUNTERPOSTURE

Return to the symmetrical version on all fours or go into the Child's Pose.

Adho Mukha Svanasana

Downward-facing Dog

adho mukha = downward-facing; svana = dog

Start on all fours, as for the Cat Stretch. Curl your toes under and spread your fingers out on the ground to help you feel stable and grounded through your arms (1). On an exhalation, raise your hips upward, pushing into the floor with your hands and pressing your heels down toward the floor, initially keeping your knees slightly bent (2). Take care that your weight is evenly distributed between your hands and feet. Hold this pose or move on to straighten your legs, with your heels continuing to descend to the floor, so that you feel grounded through your legs and feet as well as through your arms and hands, while your hips reach upward (3). To recover, reverse the path taken into the position.

Timing

Hold for four to 12 breaths.

This posture is considered to be a back bend, as you work toward hollowing your spine—your tailbone reaches upward as your abdomen is brought in toward your thighs by hollowing your lower back. In hollowing your upper back, your chest reaches toward the floor. Head and neck are held in line with your arms alongside your ears, or your chin is brought in toward your chest with eyes looking toward your navel. Remember to work patiently at your body's level of flexibility.

When you are more advanced, you can move from a Cat Stretch directly into the Dog Stretch. This enhances your ability to feel the hips initiating the movement and also establishes your hollowed spine.

Caution

If you have high blood pressure or a heart condition, this pose, being an inverted posture, should be avoided. You can adapt this position by placing your hands in a tabletop position against a wall, so that your head remains above the level of your heart.

CHANDRASANA

the Crescent Moon

chandra = moon

It is better to start with your right leg first, then repeat the sequence with the left leg forward. Kneel on all fours, with toes pointing out behind you (1). Step your right leg forward, placing your foot between your hands, with toes pointing forward and heel placed in line with your bent knee (2). If your knee tends to sway outward, aim it into the center of your chest as you move into position. Your hands can rest flat on the floor or on your fingertips. Lunge forward into your left hip, feeling the stretch in this area. Draw your shoulder blades down as you reach forward with your head and extend your spine. Hold this position.

If you feel your balance is stable, straighten up your torso extending your spine upward. Place your hands either on your right thigh, or in line with the sternum in the Prayer Pose (3), hands touching or slightly away from the sternum. To recover, reverse the path taken into the position.

Note: Chandrasana is categorized as a back bend since, in the advanced version, arms are extended to a parallel position alongside the head, and the spine is curved backward, head facing up.

Timing

Hold static version for three to eight breaths.

Bhujangasana

the Cobra

bhujanga = snake, cobra

Dynamic or static version

Lie face down with forehead touching the floor, legs and heels together. Hands are placed flat on the ground under your shoulders or next to your face (1). Inhaling, tighten into your buttock muscles (or, if advanced you can tighten into your pelvic floor muscles) to support your lower back, then raise chest and head off the ground, initiating the movement with the strength of your back and using your hands to press into the floor for support (2). Keep your elbows on the floor.

If you have a flexible spine and can attain the position using the strength of your back rather than pushing with your arms, then raise your elbows off the floor, keeping your

hands in the same position (3). Hold this pose for three to 12 breaths or continue with the dynamic version.

For the dynamic posture, exhale as you lower your torso and head back down to the floor, returning to the starting position. Repeat raising and lowering your upper body, inhaling and exhaling as instructed, three to six times before holding the static position. Extend this pose by raising your chin upward to open and stretch the front of your neck, taking care to shorten the back of the neck as little as possible.

If you have a neck problem, keep your head and neck extended in line with your spine (see 2).

Above The final pose of Bhujangasana—torso curved back and head and chin lifted—resembles a cobra about to strike, hence the Sanskrit name given to this posture.

MATSYASANA

the Fish

matsya = fish (as seen from above)

Lie on your back with legs straight and held parallel, your arms and hands (palms down) at your sides (1). On an inhalation arch your back, pushing your chest upward, aiming to raise your torso off the ground. Use your arms for support by pressing your elbows into the ground while keeping them close in at your sides (2). Your neck and head remain on the ground.

Hold this position for a breath or two, then on an inhalation, push your chest further upward, pressing your elbows into the ground and raising your torso even further. Release your head from the ground and tilt your neck and chin backward, so that the front of your neck and throat are open (3). Lightly place the crown of your head on the ground, so that your eyes look out behind you. Hold this position between two and eight breaths, then recover to the starting position.

Caution

If you have a neck problem, do the first stages of Matsyasana without involving your head and neck.

COUNTER-POSTURE

To release your head, neck, and chest, raise your head and shoulders on an exhalation to look toward your toes. Repeat this motion three times.

PREPARATORY EXERCISE

You can do this pose resting on a cushion placed under your rib cage to help ease your body into the position.

Setu Bandha Sarvangasana

the Little Bridge

setu = bridge

bandha = energy-binder that directs subtle energy flow

sarvanga = whole body (balanced on shoulders and neck)

Dynamic or static

Start lying on your back, with your knees bent and the soles of your feet on the ground, a small distance apart and parallel (1). Bring your heels in as close as you can to your hips. Arms rest at your sides, hands palms down.

Inhaling, press down on your feet and start by pressing your navel toward the ground as you begin to raise your hips upward. Then gradually allow the middle and upper sections of your spine to rise (2), peeling your spine off the ground vertebra by vertebra, until the weight of your body is shared between your feet and shoulders, with your chest raised toward your chin.

Hold this position for the static version. You can place your hands under your lower back for support, keeping your elbows resting on the ground (3). Alternatively, move on with the dynamic version, exhaling as you return to the starting position, and again replacing each vertebra one by one. Repeat moving into and out of the Little Bridge while inhaling and exhaling.

Timing

For static version, hold for four to eight breaths.

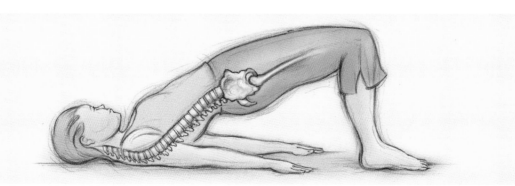

Above The gentle curving of the spine in this supported posture tones the cervical, dorsal, lumbar, and sacral areas of the spine, while at the same time strengthening the shoulders and extensor muscles of the back.

Spinal twists

Spinal twists are particularly effective for aligning the vertebrae of the spine. They give a gentle massage to the internal organs of the abdominal area and also open the chest
area, encouraging fuller breathing into the rib cage. Spinal
twists have a beneficial effect, too, on the autonomic nervous system, as they revitalize the nerve ganglia that run
from the spine to the periphery of the body. They exert a
greater influence than any other group of postures, particularly on the Vagus nerve. The Vagus is a cranial nerve of the
parasympathetic nervous system; it runs from the brain
down the spinal column, ending at the solar plexus, and
supplies the heart, lungs, and internal organs.

Postures incorporating spinal twists have a soothing
effect on the body and mind by enhancing the calming role
of the parasympathetic nervous system. They also have a
beneficial influence on a subtle energetic level—that is, on
the body's seven energy centers, or chakras. These are located at nerve plexuses in the body such as at the solar
plexus and the cardiac plexus, and all of the energy centers
benefit from the twists.

Spinal twists also have an energizing effect. Energy or
power is generated as a result of the vitalizing of the nerve
centers, releasing additional energy that may have been
locked in the body and thus freeing it for better use.

Counterposture

Apanasana (Wind-relieving Pose) is a highly recommended counterposture (see Rest Poses, p26–27) to sitting spinal twists. It helps restore symmetry to the body
and gives a soothing massage to the spine. Apanasana
can be practiced before and after spinal twists.

Cautions
- Take care if you have a spinal problem or injury;
  consult your doctor first.
- Do not jerk into or out of spinal twists or bounce
  while holding poses. Never force them.
- Keep your spine as lengthened as you can when moving into a spinal twist, also taking care to keep the
  spine centered throughout so that it forms a central
  axis for the twist.
- Ensure that weight is evenly distributed on both sides
  of your body, i.e. on both shoulders when lying on
  your back or on both buttocks when sitting.
- Work to keep your shoulders level throughout.

Benefits
- Helps relieve backache by aligning the vertebrae.
- Gives a gentle massage to the lower back.
- Helps digestion by giving a gentle squeeze to the
  abdominal organs (stomach, liver, kidneys, pancreas)
  and aids peristalsis in the intestines.
- Gives a gentle squeeze to the Vagus nerve and at the
  root of the autonomic nervous system.
- Increases sense of vitality.

*Asana is perfect firmness of body, steadiness of
intelligence and benevolence of spirit. Perfection in
an asana is achieved when the effort to perform
it becomes effortless and the infinite being within
is reached.*

—Yoga Sutras of Patañjali

GENERAL PREPARATORY EXERCISES

a

Caution

Take care not to be too rigorous with your swings; always twist gently and with care.

b

Dynamic swings

Start in a cross-legged, comfortable sitting position or sit with the soles of your feet touching, so that your legs form a wide diamond shape (a more open version of the Butterfly). Alternatively, stand with legs hip distance apart and parallel, knees slightly bent.

On inhalation, raise your arms to the sides to shoulder height (a). On exhalation, gently rotate your torso to one side, taking your head with you and allowing your arms to wrap around your hips or waist (b). Repeat, rotating your torso to the other side. Aim for a smooth, swinging movement around your spine as a central axis.

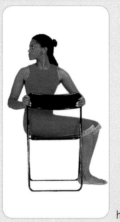

Static preparatory twist

Sit sideways on a chair that has a backrest. Start with the backrest on your right side. Place your feet flat on the ground (or on a block if your feet do not reach the ground). On an inhalation, gently rotate your torso to the right, taking hold of the backrest with both hands. Aim to keep the spine perfectly straight throughout. Turn your head and eyes to look over your right shoulder. Hold for three to six breaths, then recover by reversing your path taken into the position.

Sit on the chair facing the other way, and repeat the sequence, twisting to the left.

JATHARA PARIVARTANASANA

Spinal twist

jathara = abdomen; parivritti = turning around

Dynamic or static

Lie on your back with arms stretched out at shoulder height, palms facing down. Bend your knees, placing the soles of your feet on the floor as close to your hips as possible (1). Legs and feet should be hip distance apart and parallel. Press your navel down to the floor so that your entire spine, including your lower back, is touching the floor. Extend the back of your neck, keeping head and neck in line with the rest of your spine. Inhale; be fully aware of your spine length.

Exhaling, lower your knees to the right side (2), keeping both feet and shoulders in contact with the floor (3). Keep your hips in line with your shoulders, not allowing the twisting action to shift your hips to the side. The twist should focus on the spine as the central axis.

In the static version of this pose, hold for two to four breaths, and return to the centered starting position.

Dynamically, follow the exhalation into the twist with an inhalation as you return your knees to the centered starting position, then continue by lowering your knees to the left.

Options

The following two options are progressively more advanced than the above version, each slightly increasing the twisting action to the spine and concentrating the twist in slightly different areas of the spine.

Follow instructions as for the version above, but this time place your legs and feet together (a), so that on twisting to the right (b), your left foot naturally comes off the ground (c)—and vice versa.

Hold legs and feet together, knees drawn up above your abdomen (a). Twist, lowering your knees to either side, keeping legs and feet together throughout (b).

Static spinal twist

Lie on your back, with both legs extended and together, and arms stretched out at shoulder height on the floor. Bend your left knee, bringing your foot in as close as possible to your hip, with your knee pointing upward (1). Left foot and toes remain on the ground (if you are advanced, the leg can be hugged in over the abdomen as in the previous advanced version). Your right leg remains extended on the ground, with the foot relaxed. Place your right hand on the outside of your left knee (i.e. opposite hand to knee). Your left arm remains extended on the floor.

On an exhalation, twist toward the right by lowering your raised knee to the right (2). Turn your head to face your left hand as you do so, keeping both shoulders on the floor throughout. Hold, then recover by reversing your path taken into the position and repeat to the other side, raising your right knee to the vertical.

1

2

Continuity and a sense of the universal come with the knowledge of the inevitable alternation of tension and relaxation in eternal rhythms of which each inhalation and exhalation constitutes one cycle, wave or vibration among the countless myriads which are the universe.

—*Yehudi Menuhin, foreword to* B K S Iyengar's **Light on Yoga**

Ardha Matsyendrasana

Half twist (seated)

ardha = half

Matsyendra = name of a great Yogi ("lord of the fishes")

also, matsya = power that vitalizes; endra = mindpower

Start in a sitting position with back upright, left leg extended, and right leg bent. Place the sole of your right foot on the floor to the outside of your left leg (1). Press your right shin against the outside of your left knee or thigh. Bring your right heel in as close as possible to your left hip.

Bend your left leg so that your outer thigh rests on the ground and your left heel is drawn in close to your right hip (2). Inhaling, extend upward through the spine and head, as you place your right hand at the base of your spine on the floor behind you. As you do so, place your left arm against your outer right thigh, straightening it with the palm facing forward (3). When the position has been established, exhale, turn your head, and look over your right shoulder, keeping your shoulders level throughout. Breathe easily while holding this position. To recover, gently reverse your path taken into the position, and repeat to the other side.

1

2

3

Option

One leg (in the above instructions it would be your left leg first) remains extended throughout.

Timing

Hold for three to eight breaths, keeping your spine centered and lengthened throughout, and breathing into the opened side of your chest.

STANDING *postures enhance a sense of being grounded through the pelvis, legs, and feet with, at the same time, a sense of growing ever-taller, up through the spine and head. This grounding can assist you in correct balance. It helps in maintaining a correct stance and a sense of body alignment, where your weight is evenly distributed on both sides. This can be carried through to posture in daily life. Balance also assists the flow of the breath, which, with movement, plays a central role in the capacity for expression.*

On a psychological level, standing postures can mirror your approach to life. Perhaps your stance is rigid and controlled, allowing little flexibility or range of motion, thus restricting your adaptive capacity. Or your stance is slumped or loose, lacking core or general muscular strength to support daily posture and movement; this could reflect a lack of direction or focus. The aim is to cultivate balance wherein the body is flexible, yet strong and stable.

STANDING & BALANCING

STANDING POSTURES

Benefits

- Strengthen and tone the legs, hips, abdomen, back, and neck muscles.
- Increase flexibility in the legs.
- Strengthen and increase mobility in the ankle, knee, and hip joints.
- Increase mobility in the shoulders.
- Help create a sense of stability, ease, and grounding in a standing position.
- Promote better body alignment and even muscular development on both sides of the body, thus enhancing a sense of balance.

Cautions

- Standing postures can be strenuous. Be careful, particularly if you have a heart condition or high blood pressure, or if you find yourself straining to hold a posture. Either hold postures for a shorter period of time or stay with the dynamic version, repeating it only two or three times. It also can be less strenuous if you hold your hands on your hips throughout, with elbows pointing out to the sides, so that the work in the posture is focused on the legs and hips.
- In the event of a heart condition or high blood pressure, bend only halfway down in bending postures. You can place your hands against a wall for support.
- Check your face, throat, and abdomen for signs of tension. Also check that your breathing remains easy and regular. If you do feel strain, gently move into a counterposture and take a few recovery breaths.
- Take care that you do not widen your legs (when this is required) more than your body can maintain. You should be able to keep your heels rooted to the ground and feel comfortable in the position.
- If you are struggling to balance, practice against a wall for added support till you gain confidence in your alignment. Practicing symmetrical standing postures can also establish a sense of stability before moving on to asymmetrical postures.

Left Yoga asanas teach you to attain perfect balance on both sides of the body; in this posture, the leg extended to one side is neatly counterbalanced by an elongated torso and upward stretched right arm to the other.

COUNTERPOSTURES

These are essential for restoring balance and symmetry after asymmetrical standing postures. After doing both sides of an asymmetrical posture, return your feet and body to a centered standing position, facing forward. Move your legs a comfortable distance apart, feet parallel. Knees are slightly bent or straight. Bend forward from the hips, allowing your head and arms to hang down. A counterposture can also be introduced after doing an asymmetrical pose to one side.

Options

(a) Hang arms straight down toward the ground, relaxing your head so that it also hangs.

(b) Place hands flat on the ground in between your legs. Knees and elbows can be bent.

(c) Fold arms and let them hang below your head.

(d) Hold in Tadasana. Alternatively, move into a Rest Pose such as Savasana or the Child's Pose.

General tips for standing postures

- Focus your attention on the sense of your upper body gently growing taller, while your feet feel well rooted into the ground as you hold or move in and out of postures.
- Find a point of focus for your eyes and hold this with your gaze.
- Keep your breathing regular.

a

b

c

Starting pose

In general, use Tadasana as a starting position for standing postures. Tadasana cultivates a sense of strength and stability. It also makes you aware of how your mind and imagination influence you to sway (there is a natural tendency to sway while holding a standing posture). The idea is to resist this and so improve balance, mental focus, and willpower. Tadasana is a good way to prepare mind and body for this kind of stability before you move on to more complex postures.

GENERAL PREPARATORY EXERCISES

Arm swings

Swing arms forward and backward as in a walking motion (a, b), keeping both arms at an even height to the front and back. Coordinate the arm swings with your breath.

Alternatively, extend arms in front of you at shoulder height (c), swing them open to the sides (d), and close again by bringing palms together. Inhale on opening, exhale on closing.

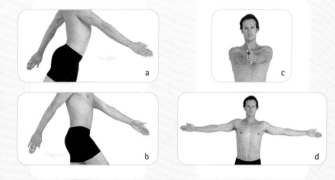

Leg swings

With your hands on your hips, shift your weight slowly from one foot to the other a few times. Then place your weight on your left leg and gently swing your right leg forward and backward, keeping it straight and using your grounded leg for support. Replace your right leg and do the leg swings with your left leg.

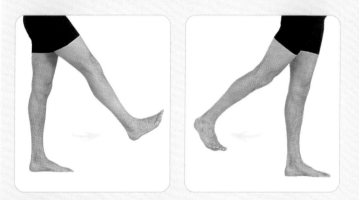

Arm and leg swings

Combine the above exercises so that one arm and one leg swing backward and forward simultaneously but in opposition (i.e. the opposite arm to the leg in forward motion swings forward at the same time).

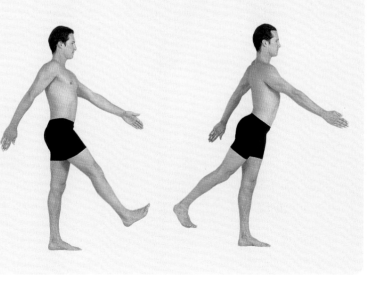

UTKATASANA

utkata = powerful, mighty, uneven

Start in Tadasana (1). Inhale while stretching your arms forward and up in a parallel line (2). Exhale, bending your knees as much as you can with heels pressed into the ground, legs and knees together, and keeping spine, chest, head, and arms in line extending diagonally upward as your torso naturally bends forward slightly (3). Hold as a static pose. To recover, reverse your path taken into the position, inhaling as you return to upright with arms overhead, and exhaling as you lower your arms down to your sides. As a dynamic version, repeat moving into and out of the pose, coordinating breath with movement. Repeat the dynamic version four to eight times in a slow and controlled manner.

Timing
Hold the static version for four to eight breaths.

Option
Clasp your hands and extend arms forward at shoulder height.

Above In Calcutta, India, a handful of Yoga practitioners limber up their muscles in preparation for an early morning class.

PREPARATORY EXERCISE

Stand with legs together or slightly apart, knees bent. Movement is slow and flowing, coordinated with the breath. On an exhalation, relax forward, lowering your head first to curl your spine downward (1), vertebra by vertebra, with the head moving toward your feet. Arms, shoulders, neck, and head remain relaxed throughout as you complete your spinal curl with the back fully rounded (2). On inhalation, uncurl your spine, reversing the path taken into the position. Repeat two to four times. You can also hold the pose hanging forward over the legs for three to eight breaths.

UTTANASANA

Standing forward bend

uttan = extension

also, ut = deliberate, intense; tan = stretch, lengthen

Start in Tadasana, with feet together or hip distance apart (1). You may bend your legs slightly if your muscles or your spine are really tight. Inhaling, raise parallel arms forward and up to line alongside your ears, with fingers pointing up and palms facing in (2). Exhaling, bend from your hips, stretching arms and torso forward to a tabletop position, arms in line with your ears. Hold for two or three breaths before stretching downward on an exhalation. Keep arms alongside your ears and keep spine extended as much as possible. Place your hands wherever you can reach on your legs; if you can, take hold of your ankles or place hands on the ground. Hold in this position for two or three breaths.

On an exhalation, draw your head in toward your legs, using your arms to assist you (3) as your elbows open out to the sides and your spine rounds over your legs. Hold, then reverse your path taken into the pose, pausing for one breath at each stage of the forward bend.

To do the dynamic version of this pose, on an inhalation immediately reverse the path followed into the posture.

Parsva uttanasana (also Parsvottanasana)

Sideways-facing forward bend

parsva = sideways

In Tadasana, move your legs apart, keeping feet parallel and heels in line with each other (1). Turn your right foot out at a 90-degree angle and your left foot in to a 45-degree angle (2). Turn your body to the right without adjusting your feet. Face squarely to the side, with shoulders positioned over your hips. The weight of your body should be evenly distributed over both legs with knees locked for stability.

Inhale and raise your arms forward and up to extend alongside the ears (3). Hold for two to four breaths. Exhale, bending forward to the halfway tabletop position (4). Hold for two or three breaths, then move into the full forward bend, placing your hands on or alongside your right leg (5). Hold in this position for between four and 12 breaths.

Recover on an inhalation, reversing the path followed into the position, and pausing for one breath at each stage you took into the pose. Then repeat to the left side.

Options

(a) Fold arms behind your back and hold elbows or forearms.

(b) Place your hands in the Prayer Pose behind your back.

(c) With straight arms, clasp your hands behind your back, raising them as you bend forward.

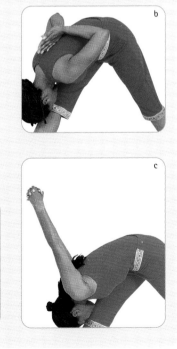

VIRABHADRASANA No. 1

the Warrior Pose

Virabhadra = a powerful warrior in Hindu mythology

Start in Tadasana. Move your legs as far apart as you can while maintaining stability (1). Keep heels in line with each other. Inhaling, raise your arms forward and up, stretching them and your hands and fingers upward (2). Keep your shoulders pressed down and your chest open. Breathing naturally, turn your right foot and leg to a 90-degree angle and your left foot and leg in to a 45-degree angle. Keep both legs straight, with heels securely rooted to the ground.

On an inhalation, turn your entire body to face the right without adjusting your feet (3). Hold for two or three breaths. Exhaling, bend your right knee, aiming to bring your thigh parallel to the ground with your knee positioned directly above your heel (4). Your right knee should point forward (not fall in or out to either side). Hold for three to eight breaths, keeping shoulders pressed down as much as possible. Keep them positioned over the hips so you face squarely to the side. Repeat to the other side.

In the dynamic version, alternate straightening your bent leg on an inhalation with sinking into the position on an exhalation, keeping your arms reaching upward throughout. If you feel comfortable in the final position, raise your chin so as to look up toward your hands, with neck extended.

Options

(a) Bring your hands together into the Prayer Pose above your head, using straight arms, with thumbs interlocked and fingertips touching.

(b) Interlock your fingers, invert your hands palm up, and stretch your arms upward.

Virabhadrasana No. 2

Face forward with legs and feet angled as for Virabhadrasana No. 1. Raise your arms to the sides to shoulder height, palms facing down and fingers pointing out to the sides (1). Inhaling, extend your spine and head upward as you turn your head to the right to look over your right hand (2). Hold for two or three breaths. On an exhalation, bend your right knee so that it is positioned over your right heel, forming a right angle (3). Both feet are well planted on the ground.

Keep shoulders and arms in a straight line, with shoulders pressed down and arms stretching out through the fingertips in opposite directions. Hips and shoulders face squarely to the front, with your spine centered between your legs. As a static pose, hold for up to eight breaths. To recover, reverse the path taken into the position. Repeat to the other side.

In the dynamic version, alternate straightening your right leg on inhalation with bending the leg on exhalation.

Below When Siva, Hindu god of destruction, was slighted by the lord Daksa, he angrily created the warrior Virabhadra (below) out of a hair pulled from his matted locks. Virabhadra went on to wreak Siva's revenge by beheading Daksa.

Utthita Trikonasana

the Extended Triangle

utthita = extended; trikona = triangle

Start in Tadasana (1). Move your legs a comfortable distance apart, then turn your right foot out at a 90-degree angle and your left foot in at a 45-degree angle. Keep both heels firmly planted on the ground to stabilize your position, and keep both legs straight throughout. Hips and shoulders face the front with your weight evenly distributed over both legs. Inhaling, raise both arms to your sides to shoulder height, palms facing forward and fingers extended (2). Keep your shoulders pressed down throughout.

On an exhalation, stretch horizontally to the right keeping arms parallel to the ground (3), then tilt sideways at the hip socket, extending your right hand in front of your right leg with your left arm stretching vertically upward (4). According to your ability, place your hand in one of the optional positions as shown. Hold for a few breaths. Look up toward your raised hand and hold in this position. If your neck feels strained, face your head to the front or look down toward your right hand.

Options

(a) Take hold of your big toe

(b) Place your hand flat on the ground in front of your right foot

(c) Place your hand on a block in front of your right foot

(d) Take hold of your shin or ankle.

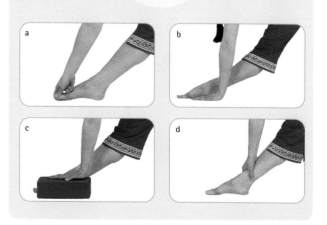

Utthita Parsvakonasana

the Extended Sideways Triangle

parsva = sideways; kona = angle

Follow instructions for Utthita Trikonasana, but start with legs wider apart. Attain the pose in which arms are extended to the sides, torso is upright, and right foot turned out (1). Bend your right knee, keeping both heels firmly planted on the ground throughout (2)—check that your legs are not too wide apart to support this. Keep your hips facing forward with your bent knee pointing directly out to the side and positioned over your heel. Then tilt into the side bend, placing your right hand flat on the ground (3) or on a block in front of your right foot (a). Your left arm reaches vertically upward so that your chest and shoulders open to face the front. Press the back of your right arm or shoulder against your right thigh to help you achieve the pose. This also helps to keep your right knee from tilting forward out of alignment with your right heel. Your bent leg should form a 90-degree angle to the ground. Hold in this position.

You can intensify the stretch by extending your left arm over your head, palm facing down. Aim to create a straight line from the outside of your left foot to your left hand and fingertips. To recover, reverse your path taken into the pose.

Move into a counterposture both before repeating to the other side and after doing both sides.

Timing
For the static version, hold for three to eight breaths, breathing into the opened side of your chest.

Options
Place your hand on a block in front of your right foot.

BALANCING POSTURES

Balance, in this context, refers to a steadiness in the attaining and maintaining of Yoga positions. It involves finding a state of ease, poise, and coordination through the equal or parallel use of the body, for example, balancing both sides of the body or balancing the top and bottom halves. It also involves finding the central axis for balance when standing on one or both legs. In this way, balance postures train and increase confidence in the body's natural sense of equilibrium, at the same time developing strength.

Balance postures work to enhance willpower and concentration. They do so by bringing you up against internal limitations that test the willpower required to maintain balance. Internal limitations may include physical, mental, and emotional experiences that may hinder your ability to balance with ease. Be gentle with yourself as you approach such limitations, frustrating though they may be to encounter. In this way, balances reveal to you how your mind literally can sway you off-center. They are thus an excellent gauge of your powers of mental focus and concentration, and help train those mental faculties while also cultivating an inner stillness and serenity.

GENERAL PREPARATORY EXERCISE

As for standing postures, use leg and arm swings (see p70) to practice balancing on one leg.

Tips to assist you in balancing

- Approach balances with minimal tension to better center yourself and achieve a state of ease, which allows the breath to flow easily.

- Find the oppositional stretch (the two-way extension) in balance postures. In an upright position, this stretch involves a downward, grounded feeling through hips, legs, and feet that is balanced by an upward lengthening from your waist, an extended spine, and a poised head. The oppositional stretch also occurs in a one-legged balance or a balance in a non-upright position, for example, between an arm and a leg that reach in opposite directions. Finding the points of oppositional extension that generally reach out from the center of your body can help you attain and maintain balance postures.

- Remember to keep breathing so that the posture feels alive. This can help counteract tension.

- Find a focal point for your eyes, holding this focus with a soft gaze while balancing.

- Be aware of both supporting leg and raised leg; feel as if you are lifting your waist off your hips so that your body feels lighter on your legs.

- If you need to build confidence, practice balances next to a wall, using it as a support.

Caution

Take care not to strain by holding balances for too long. Rather hold them for a shorter length of time initially, perhaps repeating the balance after taking a few recovery breaths in a relaxed standing position.

Utthita Hasta Padangusthasana

Raised leg balance

utthita = extended; hasta = hand; pada = foot

padangustha = thumb or toe

Start in Tadasana. Place hands on hips. Shift your weight onto your left leg, inhale and, keeping your right leg straight, raise it off the ground directly in front of you, keeping your hips level as you do so (1). Balance in the pose. Then bend your right leg so that you can take hold of the big toe or outside of the right foot (2), and fully extend the leg in front of you, keeping your left leg straight (3). Repeat to the other side, but balance for an equal time on both legs.

Natarajasana

the Dancer

Nataraja = one of the names given to Lord Siva, also known as "lord of the dance"

Stand with legs together. Shift onto your left leg and bend your right leg, taking hold of the top of your foot or ankle with your right hand; keep knees together. Extend your left arm in front of you at shoulder height, keeping your shoulders level (1). Balance in this position. Then raise your right leg as high as you can behind you, extending your right arm as you do so. Make sure your right thigh is facing downward (2). Hold for three to eight breaths. Feel the two-way stretch between your left arm reaching forward, and your right arm and leg reaching backward. Repeat to the other side.

VRKSASANA

the Tree

vrksa = tree

Start in Tadasana. Bend your right knee and place your right heel as high up against the inside of your left leg as possible, aiming to place it in your groin. You can use your hands to help position the foot (1). Your right knee points out to the side, while your hips face the front.

Place your hands in the Prayer Pose in front of your sternum (2). Balance, feeling the two-way stretch between your head and grounded left foot. Pressing your right foot into your thigh can also be helpful to your balance.

Options

After establishing the Prayer Position in Vrksasana, stretch your arms above your head with hands still in the Prayer Pose (a); you can interlock your thumbs to help you maintain the overhead Prayer Pose (b).

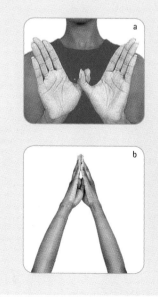

HAND BALANCES

PREPARATORY EXERCISE

Start on all fours, with hands directly under the shoulders throughout. Move one, then the other knee further back from the hips, resting both on the floor. Hold, maintaining a straight line from knees to head.

CHATURANGASANA

the Plank

chatur = four; anga = limb

(four limbs in contact with the ground)

On all fours, with hands under the shoulders and knees under the hips, curl your toes under and straighten your legs out behind you, lifting out of your shoulders. Bring your body into a straight line from head to heels, avoiding dipping the spine or moving the hips out of line. Feel the two-way oppositional stretch between the crown of your head reaching forward and your heels reaching backward. Breathe into your abdomen to avoid accumulating excess tension in this area. To recover, reverse your path taken into the position.

PURVOTTANASANA

the Inclined Plank (back bend)

purva = east (front of body)

purvotta = intense stretch of front of body

(This is a version of Purvottasana, known as Half Bridge)

Sit upright, legs hip distance apart and parallel with knees bent and feet flat on the floor (1). Arms are straight, hands at your sides. Inhaling, rock your weight onto your feet and raise your hips as you bend, then straighten your elbows, keeping your shoulders pressed down (2). Allow your head to relax backward (3) or keep neck extended by looking toward your hips. Exhaling, reverse your path to the sitting position.

Repeat three to eight times, then inhale into position and hold as a static pose.

INVERTED POSTURES

Inverted postures are an indispensable part of Yoga practice. They have a revitalizing effect on the body and mind, and also influence the subtle energy centers of the body.

On a physiological level, inverted postures enhance blood circulation throughout the body, helping to nourish body tissues. They also have a beneficial influence on the endocrine system, which influences immune system functioning. The antigravity position of inverted postures gives the digestive system a well-deserved rest, contributing to keeping this area toned and healthy. Inverting the body, too, gives a rest to the heart and increases the blood supply to the brain. This can have a rejuvenating effect on the brain cells and enhances mental faculties such as memory and motor skills.

In general, allowing the body to relax from its habitual upright stance helps counteract and alleviate bodily tension. Inverted postures help, too, to counteract the pull of gravity in the aging process. By promoting the lengthening of the spine and its elasticity, they stimulate the flow of spinal fluid and allow the nerves stemming from the spine to communicate more freely. This has a nourishing and energizing effect on the entire body, which is beneficial well into old age. The increased blood supply to the facial tissues can also slow the aging process of wrinkles forming on the face.

On a subtle energetic level, inverted postures work mainly on the crown energy center, or chakra, which is associated with the pineal gland, located in the brain. Also referred to as the "third eye," it is believed to be linked to higher states of consciousness. The pituitary gland, considered to be the master endocrine gland, and attached to the base of the brain, is also nourished in inverted postures. The pituitary regulates the functioning of all the glands in the body. The Shoulder Stand, Plow, and Little Bridge poses, create a concentrated blood supply in the throat area, nourishing the thyroid gland, which regulates metabolism.

Cautions

There are certain conditions in which inversion is contraindicated. If you are in doubt about a condition you may have, consult your doctor or health practitioner before attempting inverted postures. These are contraindicated if:

- you suffer from a heart condition
- you have high blood pressure
- you have an eye problem, such as a detached retina
- you have an ear problem where inversion is not advised
- you are pregnant; there is an exception to this only if you were well practiced in inversions before pregnancy. Even so, practice with care, perhaps using a wall or a chair for support.
- you are menstruating (unless supervised by a teacher)
- you develop any pain or discomfort in your neck, spine, or anywhere else in your body. Often injuries only occur when your body is not held in the correct alignment. It is important to consult your Yoga teacher before continuing to practice.

Timing

Hold each inverted posture for three to 12 breaths or longer if you can comfortably do so.

Yoga is the cessation of movements in the consciousness. Practice and detachment are the means to still the movements of consciousness.

—Yoga Sutras of Patañjali

Preparation for Sarvangasana

Lie on your back, with your buttocks a small distance away from a wall, so that the soles of your feet rest against the wall with knees bent (1). Keep your legs parallel and together or hip distance apart. Arms are at your sides and extended along the floor, palms down. Walk your feet up the wall (2) as you push forward in your hips, bringing your chest up toward your chin (3).

Option

In the Shoulder Stand, a folded blanket provides a soft, raised surface for your shoulders, reducing the curve of the throat and pressure on the neck.

Sarvangasana

the Shoulder Stand

sarvanga = whole, everything (benefits the whole body)

Lie on your back and bend your knees, placing the soles of your feet on the ground, with legs held together. Place hands on your hips or waist, with your thumbs pointing forward on the waist and palms and fingers underneath the back supporting it (1).

On an exhalation, swing your knees up over your abdomen, keeping your legs bent and raising your torso. The weight of your body shifts onto your shoulders and upper back. Press your elbows into the ground as your hands support your back (2). Bring elbows as close together as you can, taking care to keep your hands level on your back.

Straighten your legs so that they point diagonally upward. Hold this position, relaxing your hips into the support of your hands (3). To extend the position, inhale as you push your hips further forward, bringing your chest toward your chin. Aim your legs and torso toward the vertical (4). Once again bring your elbows closer together, pinching your shoulder blades together and shifting your hands to support your upper back as close to your shoulders as possible. Hold this position. You can also straighten your arms and place them on the ground, parallel to each other and pointing away from your head, with palms facing down (see the preparatory exercise against a wall).

PREPARATORY EXERCISES

The following exercise is good for building shoulder strength for supporting the Headstand (Sirsasana). Kneel on all fours and place your forearms on the ground, fingers interlocked and elbows shoulder-width apart (1). Curl your toes under and raise your hips upward, moving into a Downward-facing Dog stretch. Head and ears remain in line with your arms so that your spine forms a straight line from head to tail (2). In preparation for the Shoulder Stand and the Plow, practice the Little Bridge (Setu Bandha Sarvangasana).

HALASANA

the Plow

hala = plow

You can move into Halasana directly from Sarvangasana. Alternatively, start as for Sarvangasana, lying on your back with feet on the floor and hands supporting the waist. On an exhalation, swing your knees and thighs over your abdomen, raising your hips and torso, and support this position with your hands on your lower back (1). Straighten your legs so that they are parallel to the floor (2). Press your elbows into the floor to help you move your hips over your shoulders and bring your chest in toward your chin; feet are relaxed. Hold this position. If you are comfortable in the pose, lower your toes to the floor while keeping your legs extended (3). Then, if you can, extend your arms palms down on the floor behind you; or clasp your hands, pinching your shoulder blades together to help you do so (4).

Sasamgasana

the Hare

sasamga = hare

This is a preparatory exercise for the Headstand. Place a folded blanket on the ground in front of you. Start in the Child's Pose, placing forearms and hands on the ground so that hands are in line with your ears and resting on the blanket. Pushing gently from your lower spine, raise yourself onto your knees as you roll onto the crown of your head (1). Use your hands and arms as support. Then extend your arms upward, clasping your hands beyond your back (2). Contract your abdominal muscles and round your spine to assist you in holding the pose.

1

2

Salamba Sirsasana

the Headstand

salamba = supported; sirsa = head

Facing the wall on all fours, knees and legs together, place forearms on the floor as for the preparatory exercise, with fingers interlocked. Arms can be moved in a little closer than shoulder width for greater stability. Place the crown of your head on a blanket up against your interlocked hands (1).

Curl your toes under and straighten your legs, walking your feet in toward your head, until your torso and hips are raised vertically upward with tailbone or hips resting against the wall (2). Raise your feet while bending knees in over your abdomen (3), and with knees remaining bent, bring your soles to rest on the wall (4). Straighten your legs upward, using the wall as a support (5), while pushing forward in the hips so that thighs are brought in line with the torso in the vertical. Try to lift up and out of your shoulders.

When you are ready, come down in as controlled a manner as possible, reversing your path taken into the position.

Counterpostures

After doing a headstand, relax in the Child's Pose. Thereafter it can also be helpful to move into Tadasana for a few breaths before finally relaxing in Savasana.

1 2 3 4 5

IN ancient Indian mythology, Surya was god of the sun. Surya Namaskar, the Sun Salutation posture, refers to "greeting the sun" and is a sequence that is coordinated with your breathing—and often done first thing in the morning. It is a truly effective way to limber, stretch, and strengthen the body and spine. Encouraging deeper breathing, Surya Namaskar increases oxygen intake, thus improves blood circulation to the whole body. As a result, the body is revitalized, making it a good sequence, too, for the beginning of a Yoga session.

The aim of the sample sessions in this chapter is to demonstrate to beginners posture combinations, while offering easy-to-follow complete Yoga sessions to help them get on with their practice.

Six Sample Sessions

SURYA NAMASKAR

the Sun Salutation

surya = sun; namaskar = greeting, salutation

The Sun Salutation is a continuing sequence of Yoga postures that is done in succession, coordinating breath with movement. It can be practiced as a session in itself or it can be used as a warmup at the start of a session to awaken and energize you.

Aim for a minimum of three rounds of the Salutation series, working up to eight or 12 rounds. (One round refers to doing the Salutation sequence once, starting with the right leg, then one sequence with the left.)

Caution

This sequence is not recommended for people with high blood pressure or a heart condition, or any condition where inversion is contraindicated. It is also not advised during pregnancy.

Over time, aim to achieve the following:

(Step 4) Straightening your legs by raising your hips upward in the forward bend.

(Step 5) Curling the toes of the extended leg under, then straightening that leg.

(Step 6) Resting in the Plank Pose, with your weight balanced between your hands and toes.

Stand in Tadasana with your hands in the Prayer Pose slightly away from your sternum (1). Inhaling, extend your arms above your head, keeping arms parallel and stretching them slightly backward. Bend your upper back and look up as you do so, arms alongside your ears (2). Tighten your buttock muscles to support and prevent overextension of your back.

Exhaling, bend from your hips, reaching forward (3) and down to place your hands alongside your feet, with knees bent and head tucked in to your legs (4).

Inhaling, extend your right leg behind you, placing your knee on the floor, toes pointed, hands to either side of your left foot. Your left leg should form a 90-degree angle (5). Look up, raising your chin, or look down to the floor.

Retaining your breath, extend your left leg back to join your right leg. Keep neck and head in line with your spine, weight evenly spread on your lower legs and arms (6). Exhaling, bend your elbows to lower your chest and forehead to the floor, holding them in at your sides as you do so. Keep hips raised off the floor (7). Inhaling, push up on your arms and slide your chest forward until your hips rest on the floor and legs are straightened, heels together and elbows bent (8), in the Cobra.

Exhale, slightly lowering your chest while curling your toes under, then raise your hips upward into the Downward-facing Dog pose, straightening your arms as you do so (9).

Inhale, stepping your right leg forward to place it between your hands, at a 90-degree angle. As you do so, lower your left knee to the floor. Look up, raising your chin, or look down to the floor (10). Exhaling, bring your left foot to join your right and lift your torso from the hips, keeping knees bent and aiming to rest your torso on your thighs, head hanging down (11).

Inhaling, stretch your arms and torso forward and upward, keeping arms alongside the ears (12) and reaching back into a slight back bend (13). Look up as you do so, tightening into your buttock muscles.

Exhale while returning to the upright starting position, with hands in the Prayer Pose (1).

SAMPLE SESSIONS

To follow are six sample sessions of various lengths. For simplicity, one silhouette image is provided per posture, and each refers to the page number on which that respective posture is described in detail. Practice each posture at the level you are capable of, and comfortable with, making use of preparatory exercises to ensure you are sufficiently warmed up for the postures. You can use preparatory exercises as postures if this is your level of capability, using this as a way to work over time toward more advanced versions.

Also take care to make the transition between postures slowly, smoothly, and mindfully, paying attention to how long you feel you need to remain in counterpostures before moving on to the next posture. Unless otherwise specified, use counter-postures as recommended on the page where your selected posture is described in full—although these posture combinations mostly do take counterpostures into account. You may want to spend extra time in additional counterpostures or Rest Poses if you need to.

There are numerous ways to combine postures, and different schools of Yoga may have particular styles of posture combination. Feel free to create your own sessions to suit your individual needs using the Posture Summary Chart (see p39) and referring to the advice on devising a safe and beneficial Yoga session. You can also work on postures you are practicing in Yoga classes, using the book to assist you in doing these safely.

15- to 20-minute session

- *Surya Namaskar (Sun Salutation), see p89.*
- *Five minutes of Savasana.*
- *Three rounds of breathing, e.g. verbalizing Ohm (on exhalation).*
- *Brief meditation focusing on a candle flame.*

35- to 45-minute session

Focus: forward bends

Timing: 20 to 35 minutes for postures including Rest Poses. 5 minutes breathing. 5 minutes meditation.

10 rounds of Ujjayi breath in Vajrasana (static) p23, 46

Gomukhasana (optional—arms only) p47

Janu Sirsasana (dynamic then static) p50

Baddha Konasana and Supta Baddha Konasana p48

Pascimottanasana (static) p51

Upavista Konasana p49

Supta Vajrasana (arms extended) p46

Bhujangasana (static) p58

Uttanasana (dynamic then static) p72

Tadasana p18

Vrksasana p80

Savasana p26

Meditation

<table>
<tr><td colspan="2">

Focus: flexibility of spinal column

Timing: 20 to 35 minutes for postures including Rest Poses. 5 minutes breathing. 5 minutes meditation.

</td><td colspan="2">

Focus: developing strength in abdominal muscles

Timing: 20 to 35 minutes for poses including Rest Poses. 5 minutes breathing. 5 minutes meditation.

</td></tr>
</table>

	Bidalasana (without leg extension) p55
	Supta Vajrasana p46 *(arms extended)*
	Chandrasana p57
	Bidalasana (dynamic, with leg extension) p55
	Supta Vajrasana (arms extended) p46
	Supta Vajrasana (dynamic) p46

Breathing: *1 to 3 rounds of Simhasana* p24

	Tadasana p18
	Virabhadrasana No. 1 (with a counterposture) p74
	Natarajasana p79
	Supta Vajrasana p26
	3 rounds of Brahmari in Savasana p23
	Savasana p26

Meditation

	Apanasana (dynamic) p27
	Leg Raises p50
	Apanasana (static) p27
	Pascimottanasana (dynamic and static) p51
	Adho Mukha Svanasana p56
	Chaturangasana p81
	Adho Mukha Svanasana (optional— repeat previous, then this pose) p56
	Bhujangasana (static)—move via Supta Vajrasana into Bhujangasana p58
	Paripurna Navasana p52
	Savasana (brief) p26
	Matsyasana (brief) followed by suggested counterposture p59
	3 rounds full Yogic breath in Savasana p22
	Savasana p26

Meditation

1—1½ hour session		
Focus: spinal twists and side bends		**Timing:** 45 mins to 1¼ hrs for postures including Rest Poses. 5—10 mins breathing. 10—15 mins meditation.

	Apanasana (dynamic then static) p27			Tadasana p18
	Jathara Parivartanasana (dynamic) p63			Virabhadrasana No. 2 p75
	Apanasana (static) p27			Utthita Trikonasana p76
	Rolling Ball p52			Parsva Uttanasana (using centred hanging forward bend as counterposture) p73
	Baddha Konasana and Supta Baddha Konasana p48			Supta Vajrasana (arms extended) p46
	Pascimottanasana p51			Setu Bandha Sarvangasana (static, brief) p60
	Ardha Matsyendrasana p65			Halasana (using brief counterposture in Matsyasana) p84
	Supta Baddha Konasana p49			Savasana p26
	Upavista Konasana p49			**Breathing:** Anuloma Viloma (seated) p24
	Supta Vajrasana (arms extended) p46			**Meditation**

Yoga is the method by which the restless mind is calmed and the energy directed into constructive channels. As a mighty river which when properly harnessed by dams and canals creates a vast reservoir of water . . . so also the mind, when controlled, provides a reservoir of peace and generates abundant energy for human uplift.

—B K S Iyengar in Light on Yoga

1—1½ hour session

Focus: back bends

Timing: 45 mins to 1¼ hrs for postures including Rest Poses. 5—10 mins breathing. 10—15 mins meditation.

Breathing: *3 rounds of Brahmari, tapping chest (in a sitting position) p23*

Neck and shoulder preparatory exercises p54

Bidalasana (without leg extension) p55

Chandrasana p57

Supta Vajrasana (arms extended) p46

Setu Bandha Sarvangasana (dynamic) p60

Apanasana (static) p27

Purvottanasana (dynamic then static) p81

Pascimottanasana (dynamic, repeated twice) p51

Savasana p26

Bhujangasana (dynamic then static) p58

Supta Vajrasana (arms extended) p46

Pascimottanasana (static) p51

Utkatasana (dynamic then static) p71

Tadasana p18

Virabhadrasana No. 1 (hanging forward bend as counterposture) p74

Natarajasana p79

Tadasana (brief) p18

Supta Vajrasana p26

In Savasana do 3 rounds of Brahmari (without tapping chest) p23

Savasana p26

Meditation

Perfection of the body consists of beauty of form, grace, strength, compactness, and the hardness and brilliance of a diamond.

—Yoga Sutras of Patañjali

When the purity of intelligence equals the purity of the soul, the Yogi has reached kaivalya, perfection in Yoga.

—Yoga Sutras of Patañjali

CONTACTS

ASHTANGA YOGA
Websites:
Ashtanga.com
power-yoga.com

IYENGAR CENTERS
(for international directory)
Websites: Bksiyengar.com
yogadirectory.com/centers_and_Org-
anizations/international/index/shtml

KUNDALINI YOGA (3HO FOUNDATION)
(for international directory)
Websites: Kundaliniyoga.com
yogibhajan.com.

SELF-REALIZATION FELLOWSHIP
(YOGA MEDITATION)
3880 San Rafael Avenue, Dept. 9W
Los Angeles, CA 90065-3298 U.S.A.
Tel: (323) 342-0247, fax: 225-5088
Website: yogananda-srf.org

SIVANANDA YOGA VEDANTA CENTERS
Websites: sivananda.org/index.html
sivananda.org/ash&cntr.htm

USA (NEW YORK)
SIVANANDA ASHRAM YOGA RANCH
P.O. Box 195, Budd Road
Woodbourne, New York 12788, U.S.A.
Tel: (845) 436-6492, fax: 434-1032
e-mail: YogaRanch@sivananda.org

USA (SAN FRANCISCO)
SIVANANDA YOGA VEDANTA CENTER
1200 Arguello Blvd./Frederick Street
San Francisco, CA 94122, U.S.A.
Tel: (415) 681-2731, fax: 681-5162
E-mail: SanFrancisco@sivananda.org

GERMANY (BERLIN)
SIVANANDA YOGA VEDANTA ZENTRUM
Schmiljanstr. 24 (Gartenhaus), U9
Friedrich-Wilhelm-Platz, 12161 Berlin
Tel: (30) 85-99-97-99,
fax: 85-99-97-97
E-mail: Berlin@sivananda.org

FRANCE (PARIS)
CENTRE DE YOGA SIVANANDA
123, bd. de Sébastopol, 75002 Paris
Tel: (1) 40-26-77-49, fax: 42-33-51-97
E-mail : Paris@sivananda.org

UK (LONDON)
SIVANANDA YOGA VEDANTA CENTRE
51 Felsham Road, London SW15 1AZ
Tel: (20) 8780-0160, fax: 8780-0128
E-mail: London@sivananda.org

SOUTH AFRICA (CAPE TOWN)
ANANDA KUTIR ASHRAMA
24 Sprigg Road
Rondebosch East 7780
Tel: (21) 696-1821 or 696-2078
e-mail: akya@iafrica.com

E-MAIL DIRECTORY OF MAJOR SIVANANDA
YOGA VEDANTA CENTERS
Berlin@sivananda.org (Germany)
BuenosAires@sivananda.org
   (Argentina)
Chicago@sivananda.org (U.S.A.)
Delhi@sivananda.org (India)
Geneva@sivananda.org (Switzerland)
London@sivananda.org
   (Ontario, Canada)
LosAngeles@sivananda.org
   (California, U.S.A.)
Madras@sivananda.org (India)
Madrid@sivananda.org (Spain)
Montevideo@sivananda.org
   (Uruguay)
Montreal@sivananda.org
   (Quebec, Canada)
Munich@sivananda.org (Germany)
NewYork@sivananda.org (NY, U.S.A.)
Paris@sivananda.org (France)
SanFrancisco@sivananda.org
   (California, U.S.A.)
TelAviv@sivananda.org (Israel)
Toronto@sivananda.org
   (Ontario, Canada)
Vienna@sivananda.org (Austria)

INDEX

Figures in **bold** indicate that the entries appear in photographs.

ACKNOWLEDGMENTS

The publishers would like to thank Carol Francis, a Yoga teacher in the Iyengar
method, for willingly lending us her studio and advising us in our photo shoots,
and our immensely supple Yoga models Gaenor Ziegelasch, Jennifer Stephens, and
Henry Crafford. We are also grateful to Claudine of Namasté Yoga & Exercise
Wear for allowing us to use her beautiful garments.

PHOTOGRAPHIC CREDITS

All photography by Nicholas Aldridge and Ryno Reyneke for New Holland Image
Library (NHIL), with the exception of the following photographers and/or their
agencies (copyright rests with these individuals and/or their agencies).

4–5	Ernst Wrba	30	Stone/Gallo Images
6–7a	Photo Access	34	NHIL/Dirk Pieters
6–7b	Nicholas Aldridge	42	Photo Access
6–7c	Nicholas Aldridge	43	AKG London/British Library
6–7d	Stone/Gallo Images	45	Stone/Gallo Images
6–7e	NHIL/Massimo Cecconi	53	AKG London/British Library
6–7f	Stone/Gallo Images	54	Photo Access
6–7g	NHIL/Massimo Cecconi	58	ICCE Photolibrary (Dr M.A. Haque)
8–9	Stone/Gallo Images	64	AKG London/British Library
10	AKG London/British Library	68	Photo Access
11	Deykers/F1 Online	71	Hutchison Picture Library
12	British Library		(Nick Haslam)
20	Picture Box	75	Hawkes, Asian Art
28	Schuster/F1 Online	86–87	Stone/Gallo Images